# Framing Privacy in Digital Collections with Ethical Decision Making

# Synthesis Lectures on Information Concepts, Retrieval, and Services

Editor

**Gary Marchionini**, *University of North Carolina at Chapel Hill*

Synthesis Lectures on Information Concepts, Retrieval, and Services publishes short books on topics pertaining to information science and applications of technology to information discovery, production, distribution, and management. Potential topics include: data models, indexing theory and algorithms, classification, information architecture, information economics, privacy and identity, scholarly communication, bibliometrics and webometrics, personal information management, human information behavior, digital libraries, archives and preservation, cultural informatics, information retrieval evaluation, data fusion, relevance feedback, recommendation systems, question answering, natural language processing for retrieval, text summarization, multimedia retrieval, multilingual retrieval, and exploratory search.

Framing Privacy in Digital Collections with Ethical Decision Making
Virginia Dressler

Mobile Search Behaviors: An In-depth Analysis Based on Contexts, APPs, and Devices
Dan Wu and Shaobo Liang

Images in Social Media: Categorization and Organization of Images and Their Collections
Susanne Ørnager and Haakon Lund

Exploring Context in Information Behavior: Seeker, Situation, Surroundings, and Shared Identities
Naresh Kumar Agarwal

Researching Serendipity in Digital Information Environments
Lori McCay-Peet and Elaine G. Toms

Social Monitoring for Public Health
Michael J. Paul and Mark Dredze

Digital Libraries for Cultural Heritage: Development, Outcomes, and Challenges from European Perspectives
Tatjana Aparac-Jelušić

Framing Privacy in Digital Collections with Ethical Decision Making
Virginia Dressler


ISBN: 978-3-031-01188-7 Paperback
ISBN: 978-3-031-02316-3 ebook
ISBN: 978-3-031-00223-6 Hardcover

DOI 10.1007/978-3-031-02316-3

A Publication in the Springer series
*SYNTHESIS LECTURES ON INFORMATION CONCEPTS, RETRIEVAL, AND SERVICES, #64*

Series Editor: Gary Marchionini, University of North Carolina, Chapel Hill

Series ISSN: 1947-945X Print   1947-9468 Electronic

# Framing Privacy in Digital Collections with Ethical Decision Making

Virginia Dressler
Kent State University

*SYNTHESIS LECTURES ON INFORMATION CONCEPTS, RETRIEVAL, AND SERVICES #64*

## ABSTRACT

As digital collections continue to grow, the underlying technologies to serve up content also continue to expand and develop. As such, new challenges are presented which continue to test ethical ideologies in everyday environs of the practitioner. There are currently no solid guidelines or overarching codes of ethics to address such issues. The digitization of modern archival collections, in particular, presents interesting conundrums when factors of privacy are weighed and reviewed in both small and mass digitization initiatives. Ethical decision making needs to be present at the onset of project planning in digital projects of all sizes, and we also need to identify the role and responsibility of the practitioner to make more virtuous decisions on behalf of those with no voice or awareness of potential privacy breaches.

In this book, notions of what constitutes private information are discussed, as is the potential presence of such information in both analog and digital collections. This book lays groundwork to introduce the topic of privacy within digital collections by providing some examples from documented real-world scenarios and making recommendations for future research.

A discussion of the notion privacy as concept will be included, as well as some historical perspective (with perhaps one the most cited work on this topic, for example, Warren and Brandeis' "Right to Privacy," 1890). Concepts from the The Right to Be Forgotten case in 2014 (*Google Spain SL, Google Inc. v Agencia Española de Protección de Datos, Mario Costeja González*) are discussed as to how some lessons may be drawn from the response in Europe and also how European data privacy laws have been applied. The European ideologies are contrasted with the Right to Free Speech in the First Amendment in the U.S., highlighting the complexities in setting guidelines and practices revolving around privacy issues when applied to real life scenarios. Two ethical theories are explored: Consequentialism and Deontological. Finally, ethical decision making models will also be applied to our framework of digital collections. Three case studies are presented to illustrate how privacy can be defined within digital collections in some real-world examples.

## KEYWORDS

privacy, ethical decision making, digital collections, digital libraries, redaction, digitization

# Contents

# Preface

While standards and benchmarks have been determined and established for many of the more practical aspects of a digital librarian's day-to-day existence (such as basic digitization capture standards and defined metadata schemas), there are other more nuanced and complex situations that arise to test an area of the profession, which to date has proved to be largely undocumented and under researched. In this book, varying notions of what constitutes private information will be discussed, as will the potential presence of such information in both analog and digital collections. There are currently no solid guidelines or overarching codes of ethics to address such issues. Publishing private information can have damaging consequences as a result of widely disseminating this data via open digital collections. The practitioner becomes the responsible party for this disclosure through the action of sharing digital content as part of their daily work.

Once content is published onto an openly accessible platform, there are ramifications to consider as a result of the action of publication. The responsibility of this action needs to be addressed, as well as considering selected, existing professional ethical standards that can help guide better, more ethical decision making. This book will strive to lay some groundwork to introduce the topic of privacy within digital collections by providing some examples from documented real-world scenarios and making recommendations for future research. I will also include some viewpoints that speak to my particular experiences with regard to the work we do in digital libraries, through a few personal anecdotes.

An initial discussion of the notion of privacy as concept will be included, and will include some historical perspectives (with perhaps one the most cited work on this topic, for example, Warren and Brandeis' "Right to Privacy" (1890)). Concepts from the The Right to Be Forgotten case in 2014 (*Google Spain SL, Google Inc. v Agencia Española de Protección de Datos, Mario Costeja González*) will be elaborated on as to how some lessons may be drawn from the response in Europe and also how European data privacy laws have been applied. The European ideologies will be contrasted with the Right to Free Speech in the First Amendment in the U.S., and the complexities in setting guidelines and practices revolving around privacy issues when applied to real life scenarios will be highlighted. Two ethical theories will then be briefly explored: Consequentialism and Deontological. Finally, ethical decision making models will also be applied to our framework of digital collections.

Three case studies are presented to illustrate how privacy can be defined within digital collections in some real-world examples. First, the libel lawsuit against Cornell University in 2008 will be explored in the first case study, as one of only first lawsuits to go to court around a digital collection. Then, an examination of Reveal Digital's decision to digitize and publish the full run of *On*

*Our Backs*, a lesbian erotica magazine which was in publication from 1984–2006 in the company's *Independent Voices* project for a second case study. The online publication of roughly 20 years of the magazine essentially outed hundreds of women by pushing a limited-run print journal to a much broader audience. Finally, a look at a less traditional "digital collection" of images within a subreddit will be explored and considered.

Finally, a recommendation of some core values and practices to consider for digital librarians will be made to provide a usable framework in decision making and project planning. While the American Library Association (ALA) has an existing Code of Ethics in place for the profession at large, the notion of privacy in the code is more centered around a patron's right to privacy, and does not address some of the other aspects of privacy and personal information that can be relevant in digital collections. Initial recommendations will be provided as a starting place for digital librarians, modeled in part from charters and principles from related writings and resources.

As digital collections continue to grow, the underlying technologies to serve up content also continue to expand and develop. As such, new challenges are presented which continue to test ethical ideologies in everyday environs of the practitioner. The digitization of modern archival collections, in particular, presents interesting conundrums when factors of privacy are weighed and reviewed in both small and mass digitization initiatives. Ethical decision making needs to be present at the onset of project planning in digital projects of all sizes, and we also need to identify the role and responsibility of the practitioner to make more virtuous decisions on behalf of those with no voice or awareness of potential privacy breaches as result of these decisions.

# Acknowledgments

This book was very much inspired by one particular real-life conundrum, and the realization that even within a small working group of librarians with a collected 50+ years of varied professional experience, we can often consider notions of privacy, and one's right to privacy, in very, very different ways. This book also reflects many conversations over the last year with numerous individuals in my life who have entertained and inspired my quest into the grayer areas of digital librarianship. I feel we are overdue as practitioners to think more critically of the impact of our decisions to share, describe, and provide access to materials that may have potential privacy hazards.

I am very much indebted to be in a work environment that affords creative thinking and also offers research leave to pursue this particular rabbit hole. I am also fortunate to have an ever-supportive spouse who overlooks my Sunday morning ritual of burrowing away into a corner of the house to steal some rare, quiet moments in the midst of the chaos and insanity that comes along with raising toddler twins; to read about ethics, privacy, and notions of time and being in the digital world. Thank you, my love—this book could not have happened without your support in so many ways, by way of your constant selflessness and sacrifice.

Special thanks and shout outs to the following individuals in no particular order: Cindy Kristof, an exceptionally keen copyright librarian who serves as a frequent afternoon coffee companion and often talks me through the crossroads; Laurence Skirvin, who gave me the courage to pencil out the first inklings of this project one fall afternoon at the student union, and also serves as my favorite philosophical devil's advocate (even if he is not as fond of Martin Heidegger as I am); Jeff Rubin, my first boss in the digital projects realm to whom I owe so much of my day-to-day practice, and who took a chance on a young woman with a no real tangible job experience at the Louisiana State Museum in 2005; Michael Kavulic, who inadvertently inspired a major line of inquiry and the underlying thesis of this book, by way of his often sage and pensive reflections that I have very much come to enjoy; Doug Kubinski, perhaps the best-humored lawyer I've come to know this past year, who advised on everything from book contracts to left-field questions of legality and ethics within the digital library landscape; and last but not least, Kay Wise, grandmother extradoniare and one of the kindest souls who inspires me daily.

In addition, this book was also very much inspired by the research, writing, and lectures of the following individuals; Tara Robertson, who has beautifully articulated the ethical problems present in the *On Our Backs* digitization project; Daniel Solove, whose writings about privacy in the digital age are phenomenal, and my only wish is that I would have had more time to ponder and digest his writings more fully in the limted six months that I spent writing and researching for this book;

and Gene Pendleton, professor emeritus in the Department of Philosophy at Kent State University, who is unlikely aware of the impact his teaching and lectures had on me as an undergraduate art history major through his Aesthetics and Postmodern philosophy courses I took many, many years ago. As I worked toward the deadline to complete this title, I realized I would have enjoyed another year to read further into the mountain of books on privacy that remained unread on my desk, which only means that my fascination and captivation continues.

I am also grateful for feedback and conversations with the following folks, again in no particular order other than perhaps the recency of our conversation over coffee, lunch, drinks, or a phone call, when they may have unknowingly given me a particular thought or inspiration: Karen Gracy, Kiersten Latham, Peter Lisius, Kara Robinson, Haley Antell, Cara Gilgenbach, Thomas W. Dressler, Thomas R. Dressler, Lizette Barton, Jodi Kearns, and Jennine Vlach. And to the Chesterland Arabica and Tree City Cafe, where I often holed up on several frigid Northeast Ohio winter days, and who provided copious amounts of coffee to fuel this writing.

I dedicate this book to our twins, Winston and Gillian, as my views on an individual's right to privacy (and the desire for privacy) in the modern world have surely been impacted since their arrival into this crazy world in the spring of 2016. And also to our first child, whom I lost inexplicably at the end of a full-term pregnancy just a year and a day before the twins' arrival. He is ever present in my heart and mind, and I believe nothing in this world will teach you more about life and love than losing an infant, and will also irrevocably alter your entire being from that moment forward. Every day that has since passed, my heart aches without you in my life, little one.

# Introduction

As someone who has worked in the digital library landscape for the past decade or so, I have come to find an interesting quandary that has become increasingly apparent in certain digital projects that cross my desk. Digital librarians have created and strive to adhere to certain benchmarks and guidelines for many aspects of the work, such as concrete digitization, and capture standards within national guidelines such as Federal Agencies Digital Guidelines Initiative (FADGI) and also from institutions like the National Archives (such as the Technical Guidelines for Digitizing Archival Materials for Electronic Access).

Other, more subtle aspects of the job are ultimately determined by the practitioner, or may be put to a working group or committee for final decisions. Some of the more perplexing areas, such as the more complex, murkier copyright issues or potential violations of privacy as result of digitization projects, have yet to be discussed widely. Perhaps these more difficult areas are harder to navigate and also imply a certain amount of risk, and we are arguably still in the early pioneer days of digital librarianship as a profession.

The aspect of privacy in digital collections is of particular interest, since the decisions practitioners make have very real and tangible impacts on the outside individual whose personal information may be at risk of disclosing, particularly in the era of broadcasting increasingly large amounts of digital media and information within connected networks with virtually perfect "memory."[1] The decisions around whether or not to digitize and publish content containing personal information in an online arena need to be weighed and examined as to potential risk and harm to the individual(s) impacted most directly by these actions.

Digital collections represent a digital version of analog collections and holdings (or are born digital content). These are materials that may be deemed rare, valuable, and/or of high potential interest for researchers. Candidates for digitization are accompanied with a number of factors that can impact or even impede dissemination—concerns of authorship, ownership, intellectual property, preservation, privacy, and so on. One rationale around digital collections is focused on digitization as preservation for aging materials, capturing a version of the original before any further loss occurs. In doing so, it prevents further handling of the original through its digital surrogate,

[1] There is a fascinating book entitled *Delete: The Virtue of Forgetting in the Digital Age* on the notion of memory and forgetting in a digital landscape by Victor Mayer-Schönberger (2009), who poses the idea of purposefully programming forgetfulness into technology, to provide a more forgiving, fallible (and human-like) network. And others like Pekka Henttonen call for more of a life cycle model, much like physical retention schedules, to set an expiration based on the orginal intent of information or a "purpose limitation principle" (Henttonen, 2017, p. 291).

although the wide dissemination presents its own set of challenges for the digital version. Copyright is one such complex area that could prevent distribution before the practitioner loads content into a wider arena of discovery. A copyright review will often take place before ingest and has been well documented and incorporated into production workflows, while privacy reviews have rarely been discussed widely for digital projects.

As digital librarians, our jobs often combine elements of project management and a certain level of technology skills and knowledge. This position often combines the more nuts and bolts aspects of the digitization and capture processes of digital media with more conceptual ones in understanding how digital platforms work, particularly in the indexing and ingesting functions. Depending on the institution, digital librarians can often feel that we work in a relatively lonely corner (depending on the size of your institution and the scope of its digital initiatives), in part due to the newness of the profession. These services often exist in a less traditional corner of library services, and some of us may be in the midst of reaching to full potential and ultimately could still be defining roles and services.

I have worked at two different academic libraries over the past decade, as the first person with the title of digital librarian at the institution, and previous to that, as a digital archivist within a museum setting. This aspect of defining one's role is, for the most part, a very freeing position, as it allows one to come into a brand new position and help mold expectations. However, a consequence of this situation has also meant that there has been a lack of direct mentorship that is often present in the more traditional library departments like Reference, Archives, or Cataloging (and in my case, getting the library science degree before digital library classes were offered). These are areas that have many decades of experience to impart on new hires as part of the training. As such, digital librarians face some interesting daily challenges that allow for a certain level of creativity and collaboration for the individual to craft the position and find answers to new problems as they arise, but lack the same level of standardization of practice that other areas of the library may already have in place. I also feel that the ethical areas can often lag behind the practice and the real world, particularly when the especially puzzling ethical conundrums present themselves, serving to be a very important piece of the long-term conversation and identifying themselves as areas in need of more discussion and awareness.

More recently, I have worked on a few specific digital projects that have had a higher potential of materials that contain private information. This is in part due to a grant which revolves around a modern archival collection. As such, many living individuals are represented in some way within the archival collections. The grant project has led to many frequent internal conversations to define exactly what constitutes private information within our institution, a process that had not been done before with regard to open digital collections. Digital librarians are, in one regard, the final gatekeeper of the information contained within digital collections. Practitioners decide when to upload and index collections to broadcast information to a wider arena than the former offline, analog version allowed. "Exactly what information is developed and published is often the result of judgments and decisions made by numerous gatekeepers." (Mason, Mason, and Culnan, 1995, p. 264). As the final gatekeeper before wider dissemination, we are tasked with a responsibility to enforce both institutional policy (if available) and also be aware of more subtle, ethical issues that result as a consequence to our actions.

While the American Library Association (ALA) has addressed notions of patron privacy surrounding circulation records in the past, there has been a shortage of discussion and understanding revolving around the idea of privacy (and privacy violations) within digital collections at large. This has ultimately led to a disparity in practice within the profession, wherein decisions may often be made on the fly during initial project proposals and content selection regarding privacy, or perhaps not addressed at all. One of the more relatable units within the library that can be referred to for practice and policy around balancing issues of access levels and privacy is the archives. The archival community have long grappled with these issues in physical holdings, and how to best balance and determine access levels to more sensitive material (Gilliland and Wiener, 2014; Bingo, 2011; Benedict, 2003; MacNeil, 1992). In part, this is due to the fact that the originators of content (i.e., information producers) could be individuals, organizations, or families that may be unaware of the scope or existence of sensitive information within collections (Wood and Lee, 2015).

Privacy is a complex and often thorny issue present in modern society, with many varying opinions as to the scope and control of one's personal privacy and right (or expectation) to privacy. This issue is intriguing to me on a personal level since I have at times found myself in a moral conflict on this topic of privacy within digital collections, mainly between the work as gatekeeper to openly accessible digital collections, and as an individual who may have a higher level of expectation or desire of privacy in my personal life. I have been fortunate to have spent most of my professional work on projects that are, for the most part, freely and openly accessible digital collections with little to no risk of disclosing private information. The processes involved in translating analog collections into open, fully indexed digital collections is personally satifying to enable the dissemenation of information. Yet, at the end of the day, I leave my full-time job and have the option to live a *selectively* offline existence of relative anonymity in rural Northeast Ohio. I enjoy the peace and quiet that is attached to living in the remote countryside, affording at times a rather purposeful detachment from modern life. And in becoming a parent recently, I have come to realize that true sense of complete privacy, and the chance of a truly encompassing, offline existence for my children, is increasingly difficult in modern society (difficult, or perhaps impossible with the availability of a mountain of public data at the end of any Google search on any person). I share these personal aspects of my particular viewpoint here in the introduction, since I feel these ultimately play an important role in how I consider and make decisions to share information that is in the nature of the position of digital librarian. The decisions that practitioners make on a regular basis to publish and share widely content with private information will impact, and continue to impact, the lives of others as a direct consequence of disclosing information online (and, as such, my role as the publisher of information becomes the *active agent* in the transformation from analog to digital containers).

Therefore, I have, within the role my position affords, a certain authority and capability to infringe on other's privacy by posting content to an openly accessible digital platform that may contain personal information. The process of digitizing analog collections and publishing online entails that items will be captured, described, and shared broadly to anyone with a solid Internet connection, in varying levels of discoverability through processes such as optical character recognition (OCR), transcription, and other methods to further liberate information from its physical container. As mentioned earlier, librarians have created selection criteria and related guidelines that serve to inform our work and justify decision making to build both physical and digital collections. Although as some of the real-world examples will show below, we oftentimes cannot fully comprehend the full implications of online dissemination and consumption, and as such need to be more mindful and aware of potential privacy disclosure.

Furthermore, as richly complex and complicated the notions surrounding privacy issues are, the related ethical decision making can be equally tricky and problematic. Ethical conundrums often fall into various shades of gray, with no easily definable right or wrong side to be found. Related decision making cannot often be put into fixed, predictive patterns due to these nuances and complexities. Each case can present new challenges and aspects to consider, and will therefore not likely fall into predefined, cookie cutter policies and/or frameworks. Frequently, such scenarios also fall outside of the range of legality, and can pose more of a moral dilemma for practitioners. Factors of permission or informed consent of content projected for online dissemination in digital collections can frequently be absent for consultation in project planning, and should be more at the forefront. And, finally, how can professionals become more keenly mindful of the impact and consequence(s) of digital publication of information? The first step is to create a framework or model for ethical decision making. Recently, some trends and conversations in conferences such as the National Forum on Ethics and Archiving the Web and projects such as student life documentation at the Barnard Archives and Special Collections[2] can point to more ethical considerations and treatment within the profession. The world of open access can at times conflict with individual privacy.

This title will strive to address concerns from both sides of the issue, acknowledging advocates of open access and privacy. I come into this debate as a practitioner who loves connecting the end user with resources by way of the free, open digital repositories, and as an individual who very much enjoys a private existence with a selective disclosure of personal information. The topic of privacy at large has been extremely intriguing as it often inflicts a dilemma at a fundamental level personally, with the desire to continue to build free and open digital collections while respecting

---

[2] Charlotte Kostelic presented on this topic at the 2017 Digital Library Federation (DLF) Forum about informed consent and care ethics on student life documentation project.

privacy boundaries of the individual. Ethical decision making can assist in this endeavor, finding solutions to best address the right to privacy balanced with the right to access.

As van Dijck (2013) noted in *The Culture of Connectivity: A Critical History of Social Media*, the boundaries between private and public life continue to be blurred with the rise of technological innovations and infrastructures. One such innovation is the digital library or repository, releasing the contents of an offline analog (or in some cases, born digital) into a larger realm of discoverability to a worldwide audience. Digital collections within these frameworks continue to build abundant amounts of information, providing the potential of connecting relatively disparate pockets of information on any given search query quite easily through the networked infrastructures.

> *Contemporary culture is fraught with its own debate over virtualism and the contradictions it presents. We live in a world where, as a result of digital communication technologies, we are increasingly connected to each other. These technologies distribute us, extending us in profound ways* (Miller, 2016, p. 2).

This aspect of a connective, limitless virtual world of information is wherein the potential privacy violation can exist.

As law professor Daniel Solove reflects, "The amount of personal information archived will only escalate as our lives are increasingly digitized into the electric world of cyberspace." (Solove, 2004, p. 26). The availability of data held throughout an endless number of networked and connected resources is staggering; content containing private information is oftentimes posted without an awareness of the individual in question. The enormity of the information readily available, wherein lives the potential for harm, increases as the virtual universe continues to grow exponentially. Introna (1997) has framed this convergence of public and private spaces via information technologies to challenge individuals by providing "fewer possibilities for making their existence their own." (p. 272). And Pekka Henttonen (2017, p. 287) ponders if in the end all spaces are potentially public ones, when examining all the ways individuals and others create digital information constantly.

The decision point for practitioners to release private information by way of the digitization and publication of the content is the central piece that directly impacts the overall scope and reach of content. One can also weigh the prospect of a nearly perfect memory inherent to digital networks of information (or Pekka Henttonen reflects on this as Bentham's panopticon in digital format, without spatial or temporal limits (2017, p. 290)), by way of the unrelenting technical structures with full index search capabilities. This idea can be directly juxtaposed with notions of programmable memory loss in computing (as suggested in the title *Delete*), or in the desire from the individual to remove content with their personally identifiable information as an act of erasure (as in The Right to be Forgotten case and subsequent ruling in Spain). A purposefully fallible machine designed to forget is just as fascinating and complex, but it is outside the scope of this discussion. Instead, the intent at this point is to make a call to digital librarians to begin to craft a framework and model that can navigate varying levels of complexity related to privacy in digital collections, working toward a more holistic consideration of privacy in the role, and impact of, publishing digital content and information.

We will also explore some key concepts in the differing notions of privacy, and how ethical decision making can be applied as we continue to navigate these murky waters. Specific examples of how privacy may be present at different levels in digital projects will also be discussed. Recommendations will be provided as to how practitioners can better address these conundrums internally in a more conscious, concerted effort to address potential privacy breaches. Increasingly, complex questions have arisen in the ongoing publication of more and more content housed in open digital repositories. The enormous amount of information online can be overwhelming, and ultimately we practitioners need to hold ourselves accountable to make ethical decisions, and find a higher level of consistency in our role as stewards and gatekeepers of digital collections in this regard.

# CHAPTER 1

# Framing Privacy within Digital Collections

## 1.1 DIGITAL COLLECTIONS

Many early digital initiatives at an institution often begin with the easier, so-called "low hanging fruit" kind of projects as the preliminary pioneers; content that had no/little direct impact on privacy or copyright concerns (Akmon, 2010), thus relatively free and clear for online consumption. And, as Aaron Purcell (2016, p. 34) reflects, "Many libraries developed their first digital projects as a way to preserve and provide access to their unique printed or handwritten materials housed in special collections and archives departments." These particular types of physical collections are oftentimes valued by aspects of the age, condition, and scholarly and historical value. Purcell (2016, p. 46) also reflected that the more valued analog collections were the initial representatives most often present in digital collections, as they often represented the more unique and interesting content from an institution. These collections can also vary greatly as to the origin of their creation; from personal papers, manuscripts, diaries, and many other media formats, to its own institutionally generated content.

The unique collections represented in early digital projects often physically reside within special collections in closed stack collections due to the rarity or value of the content. Further, Special Collections and Archives units have long dealt with varying levels of private and public content housed within a single collection. And, as Karen Benedict (2003, p. 13) ruminates on two types of materials often found in archives, "Manuscripts and personal papers in archival repositories occupy a middle ground between public and private records." The presence of certain types of personal information in archival collections (such as social security numbers or student grades) has also often led to a common practice of redacting private information in the physical access copy of an item for public consumption. Redaction often follows internal policy or local practice as to what type of information qualifies as private data.

As we begin to think about the different origins of the physical collection, we can also start to think about the original *context*, *purpose*, and intended *audience* evident in the analog collection or item. Items may have adjoining collection documentation of donor agreements or other pieces of information relating to provenance, and perhaps even copyright transfer, intellectual property rights, and/or digitization clauses (although less likely with older collections; Gilliland and Wiener,

2014). These three aspects of the original item can be useful in decision making around privacy concerns, as we will discuss further in Chapter 3.

As digital librarians continue to venture more into the difficult projects and collections once the easier, less complicated ones have been completed, the more ambiguous and increasingly complex these concerns can become. Practitioners have the ability, and capacity, to create high-quality digital items and publish information more broadly, although this does not always mean that we necessarily should do so. (This idea is very much inspired by Tara Robertson's blog post (2016a), entitled: "digitization: just because you can, doesn't mean you should.") Purcell commented on an aspect of this when he reflected: "Why should the library digitize materials for online users? The initial answer is often because the institution has the expertise, equipment, and other resources to make digitization possible. More simply, because they can digitize materials, they do" (Purcell, 2016, p. 44). We are at a crossroads where we must better address the possible consequences of information disclosure more seriously and build this into project parameters, much like we have set benchmarks for other aspects of digital initiatives.

Another notion that Purcell touches on centers around the idea that "the content itself may dictate access, especially when personal, controversial or sensitive information is included in the [digital] collection." (Purcell, 2016, p. 147). This concept of the content dictating access is an intriguing notion, and has not been addressed in depth, or at least not often enough. In digital librarianship, we can find that the more complicated issues can extend beyond those of copyright, legal, property, or intellectual property rights and into the grayer ethical areas to disseminate content more empathetically and equitably with respect and consideration of issues such as privacy and cultural sensitivity through our work.

Further, the question of the fundamental ownership of physical collections is often problematic which can directly impact digital initiatives. Again, Purcell says, "Unfortunately, libraries and archives of all sizes have significant gaps in documenting the ownership and provenance of their manuscript and archival collections" (Purcell, 2016, p. 48). Depending on the institution and local practice, there may be a variety of approaches to an unknown, or undocumented, tracing of ownership of items and collections. Some institutions routinely take a certain degree of risk in their everyday action and resulting work, from the more cautious to the more daring ones who may push at the legal and ethical boundaries (or may later claim ignorance of the fact), as we will explore in the case studies.

As a profession, we can work to make the more ethical decisions, to find solutions that both address privacy and provide the necessary tools and framework to assist with this work for more permissive dissemination of content. And, as Reese and Banerjee (2008, p. 19) note, "the rules of the virtual realm are not as clear as the rules of the physical world (to the extent that those are clear)." and perhaps it is time to find more clarity in what we do and how we operate. In the massive digital inititives where the goal is often to digitize as much content in a short amount of time, the ease of publishing content online en masse is at a much lower bar than the review and consideration it would take in a more critical review within a slower-paced, smaller-scale digital initiative that includes an item level review.[1] The work entailed in an in-depth privacy review requires additional time and staffing for such an endeavor, particularly if there has been a minimal level of processing or description of content (Gilliand and Wiener, 2014). In general, digital librarians have acted on these early digital initiatives from the vantage point that because we are *able* to digitize, publish, and share relatively easily that we often do, and perhaps we are overdue to think more critically about these initial decisions to publish content online and their adjoining workflows, particularly as they may relate to privacy disclosure.

To begin this work, we must look to outline what we mean when we use the word "privacy" and then identify ways to resolve issues around private information present in digital collections. One idea involved in this second piece of the process can revolve around moving toward informed consent or permission, which is arguably as cumbersome and complex as defining privacy itself. If we lived in a world in which individuals gave consent for every piece of information published, one would still need to know to what *awareness*, *consent*, and *control* one gave (or did not give) for dissemination outside of the initial purpose. One example: a photograph was originally published in a small run magazine geared toward an audience of a particular sexual orientation, and is now being posted within a digital collection that is open to a much wider audience outside of the original scope. The original consent, particularly those drawn up in the pre-Internet era, did not accommodate for the notion of instantly reaching users by publishing to more openly accessible and indexed digital collections. So, where does this leave us as practitioners to make ethical decisions regarding the stickier scenarios (as Case Study #2 will show)? We can add these three factors of *awareness*, *consent*, and *control* about the information to the three elements of the item or collection that we outlined above in our review process earlier in the chapter (*context*, *purpose*, *audience*).

Modern society partially subsists within a constantly changing and adapting digital landscape, comprised of underlying tools, technologies, and ever-shifting media formats and its potential and capabilities. And as part of this landscape, digital libraries occupy a corner of this real estate, hosting massive amounts of information within many shapes and sizes of access. As mentioned earlier, this is still a fairly new territory, and as Reese and Banerjee (2008, p. 245) state, "Digital resources have existed for only a few decades, and not enough time has passed for libraries to know what formats, methods, and systems are best suited to archiving and serving these materials." I think, likewise, some of the more extenuating, long-term, and complex consequences of content published through open digital initiatives are also lagging behind when we take a bird's eye view at the practice and underlying realities of potential privacy violations.

---

1   Zinaida Manžuch (2017) discusses the challenge particular to identifying and protecting personal information in large-scale digitization initiatives in the article, "Ethical Issues of Digitization Of Cultural Heritage," as well as the inherent conflict of open access and traditional heritage objects.

## 1.2    BASIC CONCEPTS

First, let's step back and have a brief discussion of digital collections and definitions of some of the basic concepts around this discussion so far. I began working on digital projects initially in 2005, when I got my start as a digital archivist on an Institute of Museum and Library Services (IMLS) grant at the Louisiana State Museum. This position was centered around working with each museum curator, who served as caretaker to different portions of the museum collection. Within the State Museum, these collections were quite interesting and diverse—focused on everything from jazz to medical to history to art to Mardi Gras and more. Each curator selected a certain portion of their respective collections to include for digitization under the grant, with the first candidate being the jazz collection. This was ultimately the only portion of the project that was completed while I was employed on the project, as Hurricane Katrina interrupted production eight months into the grant cycle. This was, however, an interesting process to allow the professionals who have the best insight and interactions with the physical collections guide the selection for digital collections, particularly the content that is both unique and available for broad dissemination. First on the list to digitize from the remarkable jazz holdings were selected black and white photographs taken by Doctor Edmond Souchon, a local physical and jazz enthusiast who documented some of the best-known musicians in the New Orleans area around the 1950s and 1960s, characters like Louis Armstrong, Sharkey Bonano, Pete Fountain, and Muggsy Spanier.

I have since seen digital projects occur in many shapes and forms—from the meticulously selected projects as described above, that articulate and accentuate the institution's mission (that have also been scanned to specified benchmarks and sufficiently described, indexed, and shared), to the middle of the road of digital collections that may not fit into any collection development plan at all and may also not be up to technical specifications or described fully (from factors that may lie out of scope of control of the practitioner for various reasons), to the just plain bad. (Such as a campus map collection hosted within a LibGuide. Yes... A LibGuide. Oh the horror! True story.)

This topic of defining what digital collections are (or aren't) could be an entirely other book in and of itself, but I think it is important to lay out a working definition before we delve into the ethics part. During a presentation at the ASIST Midwest Regional Conference in September 2017, Terry Reese, Head of Digital Initiatives at The Ohio State University, stated "At this point in our history, there is no such thing as a digital library (or digital collections for that matter)" (Reese, 2017, Slide 6). I found this statement to be a striking one for those of us fully entrenched in the field of digital librarianship, and as I would like to interpret the statement, digital "things" are all around us, whether or not they are presented as a curated digital collection or outside of the context of a more defined, "traditional" digital repository.

I have attended a nauseating number of meetings over the years in my role as a digital project manager at three different institutions, often agonizing over selection, description, curation, and presentation of varying types of digital media hosted on a trusted and approved digital platform within a curated digital collection. But as time (and, perhaps more importantly, the analytics) has shown, users overwhelmingly come into digital repositories (or content hosted elsewhere) through single search box Google searches and could likely care less about the structure of the collection (Lown, Sierra, and Boyer, 2013; Dempsey, 2008) or overarching digital library structure when accessing the desired content. So long as the search is successful and the correct content is accessed, most individuals may not necessarily care as to the underpinnings of the platform, system, or even the organization of the digital library at large. Not that we need to discard the notion of caring about overarching digital collection frameworks, collection development policies or the concept of the trusted digital repositories, but perhaps the notion involved around the all-encompassing digital library filled with nice packages of digital things could be a little more lenient than previously considered. This ideology is in conflict with many in the field, such as Marilyn Deegan and Simon Tanner (2002, p. 26) state in *Digital Futures: Strategies for the Information Age*. They lay out the necessity of a highly managed environment that discredits the notion of the more random pockets of hosted content that is prevalent throughout the World Wide Web. These arguments ultimately extend outside of the scope of this title, but I do think that this is an interesting area to note, as we look to define digital collections (in particular, as we consider Case Study #3).

Digital collections, as a concept, are perhaps more of an enigma, a misnomer, can often be found beyond the virtual walls of the trusted digital repositories, and are present within socially and individually constructed areas online. I say this at this particular point since I believe we can extend the application of more ethical decision making discussed later to a broader scope; anyone with the ability to upload a photograph, write a blog post, make a salacious comment, etc., could be argued as creating data points (and therefore pinpoints for discovery), when these digital items are publicly broadcasted and thus made discoverable. The main scope of this argument will however center around the more traditional, curated digital collections, and the ways in which we have to date made the decision to create and publish collection on various platforms for the greater purpose access, and this is precisely where this action intersects with private data. "Privacy concerns can exist wherever personally identifiable information or sensitive information is in collections, *stored* or *used*" (Newman and Tijerina, 2017, p. 8, my emphasis). Digital libraries serve up content without bias, contingent only on the technology requirement to access content.

## 1.3    PRIVACY: MAIN CONCEPTS AND OVERVIEW

> *I give the fight up! Let there be an end,*
> *A privacy, an obscure nook for me.*
> *I want to be forgotten even by God!*
> Robert Browning, Paracelsus, V. Paracelsus Attains (1932, p. 490).

Privacy can quickly become an elusive and nebulous term when we attempt to pinpoint its precise scope and definition. This work also quickly becomes complex when we move from a broad view and attempt to drill down into the finer details and working definitions that a practicioner can apply locally, as we will explore below from previous research and literature on the topic.

Privacy is not a given, universal right. Each society views the notion of privacy from different cultural perspectives, and has set its own framework from particular societal definitions of privacy for its citizens. As Freeman and Peace reflect (2005, p. 165), "… privacy is more than just a constitutional or legal right. The right to privacy is a fundamental, constitutive norm of American democracy; civil liberties, including the right to privacy, offer important constraints on the power of the government", despite the fact the notion of privacy has no place in the constitution or early guiding documents. Privacy can be looked at as more of a personal freedom, a "core societal value of security" (Tavani, 2008, p. 157), or a "prima facie" (MacNeil, 1992, p. 3), and it can be increasingly difficult to obtain freely, or completely, in a postmodern world of connectivity, browser cookies, and readily accessible digital information. Privacy is often also reserved exclusively as a luxury afforded only to the living.[2]

As Karen Benedict notes (2003, p. 17), "The courts have held that the right to privacy ends with the individual's death." If we could come to a general consensus of a baseline privacy, and that the expectation of privacy did indeed end at one's death, this could be the point of coverage and an application for practitioners. This could ultimately be used much in the same light to which modern copyright subsists, including defined timeframes on content types as to whether an item can be copied broadly beyond its original publication and providing defined rights to the original creator. However, not all agree that privacy rights should disappear at death; as Millar (2017, p. 117) notes, "The passage of time offers the best resolution to issues of privacy."

Iglezakis, Synodinou, and Kapidakis (2011, p. 415) describe privacy as a moral right, which can be waived by the individual, but not transferred. The authors goes on to say, "Privacy is expressly recognized as a fundamental right in most jurisdictions, with the exception of the U.S., in which

---

[2]  An interesting conversation ensued on social media channels when The New York Society Library made the announcement that they had digitized and published patron circulation records from the 18th to early 20th centuries from their more prominent members such as Alexander Hamilton, Willa Cather, and W. H. Auden (to name a few), before privacy laws were in place to prevent saving this kind of information. Some librarians argue that the right to privacy should extend beyond death. Original story can be found here: https://www.atlasobscura.com/articles/new-york-society-library-borrowing-records.

privacy is considered as a penumbra right that derives from other rights." And in the 1950s, American legal scholar William Prosser described (1955, p. 643) the right to privacy as a privilege, which "is not unlimited, but the line is a most difficult one to draw." Prosser wrote on privacy in the shape of a legal tort [3] in his extensive writings on the subject examining previous court cases involving the issue (more on this later in the chapter).

Australian consultant Roger Clarke framed privacy as a basic human right that is necessary and fundamental for a healthy society. He outlines five aspects of privacy: philosophical, psychological, sociological, economical, and political. Some of his core arguments are pinned to the idea that individuals need safe, private spaces to feel free to behave, think, and move without consequence or with the notion of being observed. The area of Clarke's paper that is the most intriguing to apply here in the discussion is the privacy of personal data is whether or not the data is possessed *by the individual* or *by another party*. Clarke (2006, p. 3) reasons that the individual in question must be able to have some sort of control over this data and its use. Tavani (2008, p. 157) echoed this notion that privacy applies much more specifically to the individual rather than society at large, and further stated that when privacy succeeds, there can be a loss at a societal level, such as surveillance or other aspects that need to heed to an individual's privacy.

However, communication scholar Zizi Papacharissi poses privacy not as an inherent right, but rather as a luxury commodity:

> *...privacy defined as the right to be left alone attains the characteristics of a luxury commodity, in that a) it becomes a good inaccessible, and disproportionately costly, to the average individual's ability to acquire and retain it; and b) it becomes associated with social benefits inversely, in that the social cost of not forsaking parts of one's privacy in exchange for information goods and services (e-mail account free-of-charge, online social networking) places one at a disadvantage. In this manner, the right to be left alone, identified with private space, becomes a commodity bartered for the provision of goods and services associated with everyday life in an information society* (Papacharissi, 2010, p. 47).

This notion of placing privacy as a commodity is quite interesting, as companies of all kinds have put value on private information captured from various contexts (which will be discussed later in the section when we address these types of "information providers"). And, within the context of his title on publishing, television, radio, motion pictures, advertising, and theater in the 1950s,

---

[3]  A tort can be defined as a type of civil wrongdoing, sometimes leading to civil legal liability. Gilliland and Wiener (2014) point out, in the article "A Hidden Obligation: Stewarding Privacy Concerns in Archival Collections Using a Privacy Audit," the fact that different states can recognize very differently constructed privacy torts making it difficult to find commonality at a national level, with each state also having distinct ways in which they each consider liability in this arena, such as the difficulty in the various interpretations of the phrases "highly offensive to the reasonable person," or to have a "reasonable expectation of privacy," that can be found within the language of some torts.

Samuel Spring makes note of the scope and coverage privacy affords, "Privacy, however is a more modern right, wider than the right against defamation. It may be violated even though the person wronged has not been defamed but has been highly praised. Truth is no defense." (Spring, 1956, p. 9). The notion of truth within a privacy violation will be a factor present in Case Study #1. These notions of commodity and truth within privacy are both intriguing in how we come to regard and work with all types of private information.

And one other aspect that Roger Clarke (2006, p. 5) draws attention to is the difference societally that we have toward privacy, calling the U.S. an "economic-technological" approach, while Europe is more geared toward broader "social values" of the individual. He further highlights that the U.S. has to date avoided any concrete, comprehensive laws to regulate for privacy, resulting "in frequent, knee-jerk legislation on specific issues." While the term privacy is absent from the Constitution, it has been heavily valued over time within the U.S. Many scholars have noted the inherent conflict between privacy and national security, and often in our culture that security has won out (particularly in the post 9/11 landscape). To date, the European Union (EU) is also more geared to protect the individual with more acutely designed data protection laws (1995 Data Protection Directive, later replaced by the General Data Protection Regulation, enacted in the Spring of 2018).

And perhaps most intriguing, law professor Bart van der Sloot speculates the following.

> *Privacy aims at avoiding norms, whether they be legal, societal, religious or personal. Privacy should not be regarded as a value in itself, but as a tactic of question, limiting and curtailing the absoluteness of values and norms. If this concept of privacy is accepted, it becomes clear why the meaning and value of privacy differs from person to person, culture to culture, and epoch to epoch. In truth, it is the norms that vary; the desire for privacy is only as wide or small as the values imposed* (van der Sloot, 2016, p. 121).

This idea of a customable, personal framework in which we both question and define privacy not as an absolute is important. Instead of regarding privacy as a finite value, we can keep in mind this malleable nature, in its varying degrees of complexity, dependent on the scenario and context define in the lens of the individual. This may be the most helpful way to reflect on privacy at large as both a concept and as an application; not on hard absolutes of what does or does not constitute as privacy, but rather an investigation and consideration of the particulars of each case, framed as a "tactic of question." For practitioners, we would still need to find the intersections where we agree on the most egregious privacy violations, yet it is important to keep in mind that our personal reflections will likely never perfectly overlap. In this type of approach, we can continue to question and frame privacy continuously, adapting as needed to changing social and cultural landscapes (and also adapt to future data policies or regulations) through systematic review cycles.

Libraries organize collections of all shapes and sizes: published/unpublished works, bound material, manuscripts, newspapers, images, audio, video, etc. There is potential for an individual's private information to be contained within any of these formats in varying degrees. And perhaps until it is shared more widely through digital surrogacy, the privacy factor could be relatively unknown or unaddressed until that point in time. The security breach or invasion of privacy may go undetected until after the infringement is made. Frické, Mathiesen, and Fallis conducted an ethical reading of the Library Bill of Rights and reflected as follows.

> *An argument can be made that even some items that might inform or enlighten should be censored. For example, there is some information that should be kept out of libraries, not because the information is objectionable, but because merely disseminating it, or facilitating access to it, would violate rights or have bad consequences* (Frické, Mathiesen and Fallis, 2000, p. 476).

This point of violating privacy or the potential of inadvertent negative consequences is at the core of our discussion.

And within the library context, archivists have perhaps been the most keenly aware of the possibility (or probability) of private information being contained in a collection. Archivists have developed solid frameworks that define usage and access to closed collections that may have sensitive information that may already be in place within an institution. Within a specific archive, these often are internal guidelines and practices to outline these practices and internal policies (Gilliland and Wiener, 2014), but digital librarians have to date not made the same considerations applied to digital collections at large, at least not in a way that is consistent or publicly discussed within the community. There are methods to restrict access or set embargo periods to digital objects, which may need to be addressed with regard to privacy issues.

The subject of privacy in digital collections has become more apparent in recent years as digital initiatives continue to grow and develop in volume, in part due to more items and the improvements in technology to more accurately optimize items for discoverability through improved OCR and transcription to provide full text searching. The boundaries of public and private spheres continue to be pushed, as each of the selected case studies will expound on different aspects.

In other literature on the general topic of privacy in libraries, the focus has often been on online behavior/surveillance using library resources and patron privacy (Newman and Tijerina, 2017; Chmara, 2009), so we must look at other areas of research. There has been very little published to address the scenario of privacy specifically for digital libraries, who are often confronted with within their daily work. And speaking from the U.S. point of view, there has largely been a lack of law to specifically and concisely address the individual's right to privacy in their public digital persona. The Privacy Act of 1974 is perhaps the closest piece of law that Americans have to protect personal information. The act required that personal information cannot be used for a different purpose without notice to the subject *and* the subject's consent. There are elements that hit on privacy issues within other laws, policies, and clauses that address varying degrees of privacy and privacy information, such as Family Educational Rights and Privacy Act (FERPA) of 1974, Health Insurance Portability and Accountability Act (HIPPA) of 1996, Video Privacy Protection Act (VCPA) of 1988, Electronic Communications Privacy Act of 1986 (ECPA), Telephone Consumer Protection Act (TCPA) of 1991, Driver's Privacy Protection Act (DPPA) of 1994, Children's Online Privacy Protection Act (COPPA) of 1998, and the Gramm-Leach-Bliley Act (GLB) of 1999.

Outside of the U.S., we can see more work on protecting the individual citizen through different data protection laws. In the United Nations, there has been work on this issue from the 2016 General Assembly publication of "The Right to privacy in the digital age: resolution," A/RES/68/167 (U.N. General Assembly, 2016). The European Union also have more coverage on this topic under the data protection directives mentioned earlier, and likewise Canada has multiple privacy statutes (both federal and regional) addressing personal information and data protection (The Federal Personal Information Protection and Electronic Documents Act (PIPEDA); Alberta's Personal Information Protection Act; British Columbia's Personal Information Protection Act; and Québec's An Act Respecting the Protection of Personal Information in the Private Sector—collectively, Canadian Privacy Statutes. In Europe and Canada, these specific laws have addressed the factors present in a digital society and largely serve to protect individuals from potential privacy violations.

## 1.4    VIOLATION OF PRIVACY

Privacy violations are at their core an exposure of personal information—pushing private information from a protected arena (physical or digital) and exposing it within a less protected framework. Or, as Frederick Davis wrote in 1959, the invasion of privacy can be defined as "*a complex series of fundamental wrongs*" (Davis, 1959, p. 20, my emphasis). The action of invading privacy is an aggressive action, even if this action is deemed to be unintentional. As Daniel Solove writes, "Privacy is about concealment, and it is invaded by watching and by public disclosure of confidential information." (Solove, 2004, p. 42) It may therefore be easier, in some regards, to define what constitutions as a privacy violation rather than making an attempt to define privacy.

In the Law of Torts, William Prosser (1955, p. 17) outlines four basic forms of invasion of privacy that were inferred from an extensive review of previous court cases, orginally published in the early 1940s. These are:

1. intrusion upon the individual's seclusion or solitude, or into his or her private affairs;

2. public discourse of embarrassing private facts about the individual;

3. publicity that places the individual in a false light in the public eye; and

4. appropriation, for another person's advantage, of the individual's name or likeness.

While dated, Prosser's outline of privacy invasion is still quite useful today particularly in the first and second forms, by way of the potential of concealed information within the analog container that had not previously been distributed widely, as we will discuss in the next chapter. The act of disclosing information into a new arena of discovery through digital collections can lead to the intrusion upon the individual, whether an intentional awareness of this information or not.

We can also examine services like Spokeo, PeopleFinder, or MyLife, the so-called "information brokers" that pull in data from all kinds of publicly available databases and other resources to combine this information and create individual profile pages without the knowledge or consent of an individual (or, "omnibus information providers", as Helen Nissenbaum (2010, p. 45) refers to these types of companies). These companies and others earn revenue by pulling together massive quantities of publicly accessible data, and charging interested parties to access in-depth profile reports on individuals that are available upon payment. While these services can be found to fall within a valid legal purview by collecting readily and publicly available information of all shapes and sizes (information from a slew of available government, state and city databases and resources that include court records, property records, etc.), there are certainly some ethical concerns on the act of compiling this information and charging for full access. The existence of these types of services does support the idea that absolute privacy in this day and age is exceedingly difficult, if not impossible. These kinds of services feed from openly available personal information, often weaving together disparate pieces of information and re-purposed into another use, and in so the potential of misuse. Woods and Lee (2015, p. 2) pointed specifically to publicly available government documents as being "sources of inadvertantly leaked sensitive information."

Mason, Mason, and Culnan talk about the power of collection of such services.

> *Large personal information data banks permit the selling, aggregating and reshaping of personal information in many new forms unanticipated by the giver who originally provided the information. Commercial practices continually challenge the definition of what is to be considered private information* (Mason, Mason, Culnan, 1995, p. 172).

Some of these services have a method for an individual to opt-out from having one's information posted and included, although this notion requires an awareness in the first place of the collection and as an afterthought once content with potentially private data has already shared on an individual. As these "digital dossiers" (as Daniel Solove refers to them) grow in their depth and breadth, it becomes exceedingly more difficult for the individual to maintain a level of privacy when there has been a collection of information.

Helen Nissenbaum reflects that many may be unaware as to the level and breadth of information already available at wide dissemination.

> *Generally, people are unnerved to discover they are "known" when they enter what they believe to be a new setting; we dislike when others know more about us than we want*

*to or when they draw unjustified conclusions about us; we enjoy sometimes escaping the demands of everyday life; and we do not like being surprised at knowledge others have about us* (Nissenbaum, 2010, p. 50).

The author goes on to talk about the role of balance in a democracy within public records and readily available information, finding the point of openness required within a democratic government and society. The notion here is to find and strike a balance between privacy and open society; a deceptively difficult task, of protecting private personal data while also providing a certain level of transparency within government and society.

The concepts of security and privacy are heavily dependent on the other, in that one assumes a level of security to protect and safeguard private information. If we look to the social media landscape as an example, an imbalance of security and privacy was seen in recent years by the emergence of the "shadow profile" on Facebook (Knibbs, 2013), and in the major violations of privacy by the capture and analysis of private user information in the Facebook/Cambridge Analytica scandal (Granville, 2018). A discovery of the shadow profile revealed that private information such as phone numbers, email addresses, and other pertinent information were copied from the Contacts information in users' phones and incorporated into these "shadow profiles," when the "Find My Friends" feature was used, deemed to be a "bug" by Facebook developers.

Perhaps the most disturbing (and the most invasive) aspect of this security breach is that there was no point of *awareness* or *consent* by the impacted individuals to glean this information. The scope and depth of a security breach in the millions of Facebook accounts meant that massive amounts of private information was used without permission and compiled into a large network of private information. Two years prior, an Irish advocacy group had shed light on this same practice that also impacted non-Facebook users, whose contact information was also compromised through the Contacts list of their Facebook friends. And, in the recent Cambridge Analytica example, a private political data firm obtained private information from over 50 million Facebook users and used this information in the 2016 U.S. presidential campaign. The private data obtained, which included many types of information from user "likes" and associated friend networks, was used to focus advertisements to target audiences. These two examples reiterate the need for more *consent* and *awareness* of the use and re-use of private information, although one can see that these violations can take place without one being cognizant of these activities. Knibbs reflects on the shadow profile scenario:

*Though the decision to publicly own up to the bug was a step in the right direction, this leak is disturbing because it illustrates just how* little control *we have over our data when we use services like Facebook. And it illustrates that Facebook isn't apologizing for collecting information—it's just apologizing for the bug* (Knibbs, 2013, p. 2, my emphasis).

If we step back and return to the digital library scenario, at the core of the conversation remain the main factors of *context*, *purpose*, *audience*, *control*, *consent*, and *awareness* that can assist and inform in the dialogue of privacy. Technology is the linchpin here, and plays a huge role in disseminating information quickly and easily, diminishing or completely removing any barrier that previously hindered immediate access to content. And as Miller (2016, p. 27) reflects, the use of technology in modern society has created a crisis in how an individual exists in the world compared to how we actually exist through the use of ubiquitous communication: "technology is a kind of medium which reveals the world to us in a particular way and that particular way is historically contingent on our philosophical foundations." We will explore the role of technology later in the chapter.

Moreover, Miller speaks of the importance of context,

> *...even data in the "public domain," has to be considered within the contexts of the autonomy of the person who articulated those thoughts and preferences. It would be unjust, no matter the level of abstraction, to take a person's words or images and use them in ways which they would not approve or which could do them harm, especially when they have not consented to their use. Data needs to retain the social context of the person of its origin in order to be treated ethically* (Miller, 2016, p. 71).

Further, researchers like Ricardo Punzalan at the University of Maryland, Michelle Caswell at University of California (Los Angeles), and Zinaida Manžuch at Vilnuis University have looked specifically at issues apparent within the context and significance in digital collections that focus on ethnographic populations, navigating difficult aspects of permission and value (Punzalan, 2014; Caswell, 2014; Manžuch, 2017). Writers like Gilliland and Wiener (2014) pose the question of scenarios that may have quasi-legal confidentiality concerns, such as collections containing information with older human subject research that would under modern review be subject to an Institutional Review Board.

Strauß (2017a, p. 260) views privacy a little differently: "...privacy defines a state where an individual is free from interference." As professionals, we can work toward an interference-free landscape on behalf of the individual, in setting a framework that provides clear and elicit categories of what should constitute as offline, private information and what would conversely be data that would not be deemed damaging or intrusive. And Strauß (2017a, p. 260) also speaks to a level of trust in society to protect privacy: "...privacy is also linked to the trust that others respect private life and do not intrude into it against the individual's will." This notion speaks to the level of awareness and mindfulness toward another's right to privacy that should be considered when publishing content and needs to be addressed more fully—we can no longer claim ignorance on the matter.

Academic librarian Dorothea Salo notes that a " [privacy] violation is inadvertent! And often involves some illegality" (Salo, 2013, Slide 2). Ever-changing privacy policies also are a part of this problem, in the attempt to pinpoint exactly what constitutes a breach in privacy is difficult when the policies and social definitions of what could constitute as a violation can change over time. "The boundaries and normative idea of privacy is constantly changing in this era of interconnectivity where information sharing and gathering in the public domain is easy" (Akpojivi, 2017, p. 281). In addition, the ease of both uploading and later accessing content is so commonplace that perhaps we need to be reminded of the lasting impact of the decision to publicly share information of any kind on a broader scale of access, both within trusted, private networks and an open platform.

Lastly, Solove reminds us that a privacy violation may not even be centered around a particular revelation of information at all: "Privacy can be infringed even if no secrets are revealed and even if nobody is watching us" (Solove, 2004, p. 44). This can support an idea of privacy by design and as a default value, as in ISO 15489-1[4] suggests. We will first need to address the role of an assessment of privacy as part of defining project parameters, which can be another compelling takeaway for project managers to apply at the onset of any digital project.

## 1.5    TYPES OF PERSONAL DATA

At this point, it would be useful to drill down more in detail, moving from the conceptual idea of privacy, and try to define some more concrete notions and examples of what constitutes personal data. While not a definitive list, it is important to begin a process of making some initial identifications of what constitutes personal data, and conversely what does not. The discussion here will be helpful for practitioners to apply locally in practice, in the hope of becoming more mindful of potential privacy aspects.

Personally identifiable information (PII) or sensitive personal information (SII) are terms that have been used in legal scenarios. The National Institute of Standards and Technology (McCallister et al., 2010) put together the following list to indentify PII with some qualifiers in parentheses:

- full name (if not common);

- home address;

- email address (if private from an association/club membership, etc.);

- national identification number (e.g., Social Security number in the U.S.);

---

[4]    ISO stands for the International Organization of Standarization, an independent and non-govermental organization that provides common standards for everything from technology, food safety, manufactured products, healthcare, and agriculture.

- passport number;

- vehicle registration plate number;

- driver's license number;

- face, fingerprints, or handwriting;

- credit card numbers;

- digital identity;

- date of birth;

- birthplace;

- genetic information;

- telephone number; and

- login name, screen name, nickname, or handle.

There is a list of secondary information that, when used in conjuction with other pieces of information, can be used to make an identification:

- first or last name, if common;

- country, state, postcode or city of residence;

- age, especially if non-specific;

- gender or race;

- name of the school they attend or workplac;

- grades, salary, or job position;

- criminal record; and

- web cookie.

Schwartz and Solove (2011, p. 1817) argue for two distinguishments to be made along these lines of identifying PIIs, in the clearly "identified" vs. the "identifiable." For our purposes here, we will focus on the more simplistic identification of PII, but this is an intriguing aspect to consider, particularly if these elements necessitate different treatment.

There are also categorical approaches to identifying personal information. In the first example below, Tavani (2008, p. 135) outlined four broad areas to categorize private data:

1. physical/accessibility;

2. decisional;

3. psychological/mental; and

4. informational.

This categorization is helpful in isolating and identifying data by its purpose, particularly as the first and third categories may have existing restrictions in the U.S. through HIPPA laws, which will be outlined later in the chapter. An initial step for practitioners can be a physical review of candidates for digitization, first passing through and flagging potential privacy hazards with these types of broader categories to alert digitization staff (or others) to complete a more thorough, in-depth review of privacy at a later point in time.

In the EU, the Data Protection Directive provides a definition of "special categories of data" containing specific areas of personal data that receive additional consideration and protection, to include: "racial or ethnic origin, political opinions, religious or philosophical beliefs, trade-union membership and the processing of data concerning health or sex life" (Article 8, Data Protection Directive). As Kulk and Borgesius note, oftentimes these pieces of information could be readily available online in many different contexts, in relatively inconspicuous avenues. The authors provide some examples, such as: a publicly posted image of someone in a wheelchair who is also identified by name, divulging an aspect of a health/medical information; or a photograph of a Catholic choir with identifying names on a church website that would reveal religious belief (Kulk and Borgesius, 2018, p. 29). Also to keep in mind when thinking about cultural differences, is that personal data could be defined and reflected on quite differently. One example can be found in Dutch law considering information about criminal convictions to be protected as sensitive data (Section 16, Dutch Personal Data Protection Act), while in the U.S. it can often be exceedingly easy to obtain detailed information about a criminal past. Further, such a review of personal data should also note the *purpose* and *context* of each piece of information, and if this was initially produced into a public or private sphere.

Another practical breakdown of categorizing personal data more specifically can be found in Kaliya Young's presentation entitled "Ethical Market Models in the Personal Data Ecosystem" at the 2015 Grace Hopper conference. Similar to Tavani's model but more comprehensive, Young provided a very useful graphic that illustrates many types of personal data, classified into ten broad categories (Figure 1.1): activity; asset data; communications; context; content; ePortfolio; government records; health data; identity; and relationships.

# Types of Personal Data

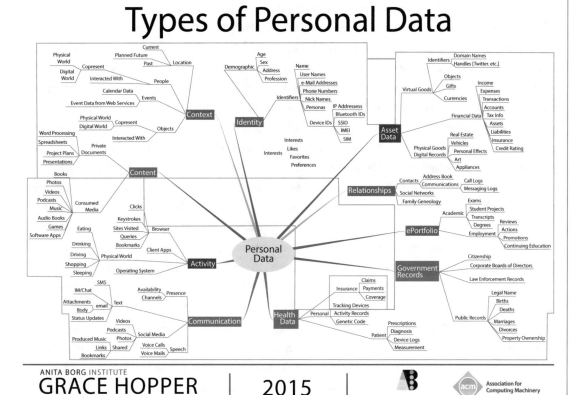

Figure 1.1: Slide 4-Young, Ethical Market Models, Top Tier information categories: https://www.slideshare.net/Kaliya/ethical-market-models-in-the-personal-data-ecosystem.

These categories are broken down further into more specific, granular areas, including both the tangible and intangible aspects. Further, Figure 1.1 can serve as part of a framework for practitioners to begin identifying the more problematic areas of private information, by indentifying the adjoining category to assist in decision making. The final decisions as to whether these pieces of information are ultimately deemed private would be a point for further conversation and discussion within the local institution.

Some elements in Young's graphic are more easily identifiable pieces of data while some are more conceptual; with some of the more conceptual exemplified in the activity section of eating, drinking, and shopping. The breakdown in the types of data within the ten broader categories is useful in isolating the purpose and underlying meaning of the information as it relates to the individuals at many different levels, as both physical and digital beings. Finally, some of Young's categories are more applicable than others in the digital library scenario.

To begin the review, both health data and student records as covered in Young's chart under ePortfolio and Health Data are two areas that have federal protection (at least in the U.S.) under the existing protection of information under HIPPA and FERPA laws. These laws specify *who* and *how* your health or student record information can be accessed with a series of protective clauses. Under HIPPA, patient medical records and other health information (past, present, and future) are protected as a covered entity, in addition to the provision of healthcare to the individual as well as payment information of healthcare to the individual. Some exceptions apply to a limited number of situations (to the individual in question: treatment, payment, and health care operations; opportunity to agree or object; incident to an otherwise permitted use or disclosure; public interest and benefit activities; limited data set for the purposes of research, public health, or health care operations). Young has added the distinguishment within the ePortfolio category between personal (tracking devices, activity records, and genetic code), patient (prescriptions, diagnosis, device logs, measurement), and insurance (claims, payments, and coverage). These pieces of information would by and large always be protected within U.S. jurisdiction during the individual's life.

Under FERPA, unless certain permission or conditions are met, any personally identifiable and directly related record with student information or any record maintained by an educational agency or institution cannot be disclosed. These records can include grade information, a student's name, identification number, date of birth, and other pieces of information, in both paper and digital format. This applies to both currently enrolled students as well as graduates (Solove, n.d.). Young classifies this information under ePortfolio, which is divided between academic and employment. Further refinements under the academic category include: exams, student projects, transcripts, and degrees. Under employment, refinements include: reviews, actions, promotions, and continuing education. Within public institutions, however, some information in Young's refinements for employment may be considered public record and as such are accessible by a public records request. This is particularly the case for some of the higher administrative positions (such as performance reviews and personnel actions), after a specified point in time. For these two specific areas (health and student records), these pieces of private information are relatively easy to define and identify.

In government records, Young lists four main areas of information: citizenship, corporate, law enforcement records, and finally public records. Public records are further defined to include the following; legal name, births, deaths, marriages, divorces, and property ownership. As discussed earlier, the public records in particular may be pieces of information that are readily available within a number of open databases and other information banks, and could justifiably be considered unrestricted information within this point of time in this (American) society. The citizenship, corporate, and law enforcement records may fall into different levels of protection, depending on the country of origin (as noted, the difference in Dutch law with criminal records being protected).

Of all of Young's categories, the Relationships category is an intriguing one to consider. The category is divided into three main categories: contacts, social networks, and family genealogy.

Under contacts, further refinements of the address book and communications is made, with sub-categories of call logs and messaging logs under communication, likely all to be considered private considering the context. Social networks have their own privacy controls (trustworthy or not), and have been reflected on ethically in recent conferences such as the National Forum on Ethics and Archiving the Web and in documents such as the "Ethical Decision making and Internet Research: Recommendations" from the Association of Internet Researchers Ethics Committee (Markham and Buchanan, 2012). Under genealogy, many pieces of information have been made publicly accessible in other avenues of research, such as name, date of birth, and other biographical pieces of information.

Asset Data contains three larger categories of virtual goods, financial data and physical goods digital records. Under virtual records, there are four categories of identifiers, objects, gifts, and currencies. And further defined under identifiers is domain names and handles. Under financial data, there are the following subcategories: income, expenses, transactions, accounts, tax information, assets, liabilities, insurance, and credit rating. Lastly, under physical goods digital records, there are the following subcategories: real estate, vehicles, personal effects, art, and appliances. Certain elements here may be considered public data; such as domain names, handles, real estate, and income (say, if one is a state employee). Other elements fall into protected private areas, such as financial data and part of the physical goods subcategory.

The next category is Communications, with four main categories: presence, text, social media, and speech. Presence has two further refinements of availability and channels. Text has four refinements of SMS, IM/chat, email, and status updates. Social media has four refinements of videos, podcasts, photos, and "shared." This final category of "shared" has three further refinements of produced music, links, and bookmarks. Finally, speech has two main categories of voice calls and voicemails. Again in this larger category, there are varying levels of whether some of this information is readily available within a publicly accessible in some shape or form depending on permissions. Presumably, unless permission has been given otherwise, most of this category would be considered protected data.

Under the Activity category, there are four initial categories of browser, client apps, physical world, and operating system. Within the browser, there are five further refinements of clicks, keystrokes, sites visited, queries, and bookmarks. Under physical world, there are five further refinements of eating, drinking, driving, shopping, and sleeping. The interesting aspect of this category is the inclusion of activities, of our physical habits that we as human beings produce by default of daily existence and being. The subcategories here would again be dependent on permission, but would in most cases fall into a private landscape. (An interesting argument here would be the digital activities within a public setting, such as a computer station at a public library.)

Context has four categories of location, people, events, and objects. Location includes three refinements of current, planned future, and past. People is further defined as "copresent" and "interaction with," with further refinements of "copresent" of the physical vs. the digital world. Events is refined by calendar data and event data from web services. Lastly, objects is further refined as "copresent" and "interacted with," also with a further refinement of the physical vs. digital world under "copresent." This category is interesting in the refinement of current, planned future, and past, as conditions and values for assessment. Context is likely to be a split category of public and private data as well, depending on the outlying factors. One could, for example, set permissions on a calendar to be public; likewise, location, people, and events could all be broadcast publicly.

Finally, Identity has three key categories of demographic, identifiers, and interests. Demographic has four further refinements of age, sex, address, and profession. Identifiers has seven refinements of name, user names, email addresses, phone numbers, nicknames, personas, and device IDs. Device IDs has five further refinements of IP addresses, Bluetooth IDs, SSID, IMEI, and SIM. And interests has four further refinements of declared, likes, favorites, and preferences. Some of the information in this category can also be obtained from public sources, much of which is also the primary information included in the information brokers that we discussed earlier. Certain pieces of demographic information are elements that may be available through other public records, and could be considered public. Identifiers and interests will likely also have a mix of privacy levels throughout, dependent on context.

Practitioners can use Young's categories and refinements as a starting place and guide to consider all the varieties of personal types of data in a more granular method than Tavani's model, identifying especially problematic areas. Practitioners could then decide which pieces of data are ones to protect, identify its context, and determine how the information relates in an individual's personal ecology of data, within a larger application of digital collections.

## 1.6    DEFINING PERSONAL DATA

I have often thought the notion of defining and controlling one's privacy is akin to a personal invisible forcefield or protective bubble, where one has chosen how much information to conceal and conversely what to make public. This would ultimately be an adaptive, protective bubble for the individual, providing a personalized and permissive definition of privacy for each individual, as distinctly as we each qualify private data. Moore refers to this concept as a shield, with the ability of one to control the level of personal information that is disclosed. Likewise, Nissenbaum has used the term "contextual integrity" that addresses the extent and method of information flow within a defined setting or situation. In 1995, before the real impact and implication of an endless network of information was better understood, writers Mason et al. (1995, p. 172, my emphasis) reflected: "If systems filled with personal data are allowed to proliferate, then ease of obtaining personal data *effectively reduces the privacy safety zone* of the individual." And in our role as digital gatekeepers, we can profoundly add to this growing bank of easily attainable personal information though our daily work, perhaps with or without awareness of doing so.

## 1.7    CONCEALMENT/UNCONCEALMENT

The specific notions of concealment and "unconcealment" are words that philosopher Martin Heidegger frequently used in many of his writings. In "The Question Concerning Technology," Heidegger talks about the general idea of technology to be a revealing, unconcealing one. "Technology comes to presence in the realm where revealing an unconcealment take place, where alethia, truth, happens" (Heidegger, 1954, p. 319). At the time of the essay (originally delivered as a lecture entitled "The Enframing" on December 1, 1949 to the Bremen Club), Heidegger's notion of modern technology would be a far cry from that of the 21st century context, but there are some particularly relevant and important applications of this lecture/essay to consider here.

Heidegger used the word technology as an all-encompassing term in the essay, as seen in his era in the industrialization that was apparent in agriculture, hydroelectric plants, and aeronautics. Quite a different landscape as we consider the digital library landscape, but I would argue there remains the core elements in Heideggers' original thesis that very much relate here: man and machine. Heidegger stated that technology can be said to be a means to an end, but only if in the same definition that would hold that technology is a human activity. "Everything depends on our manipulating technology in the proper manner as a means" (Heidegger, 1954, p. 313). Echoed here is the role of man, as the instigator and inventor, and also the entity which is responsible for consequences of action, or what can be referred to as the active agent.

The two issues of control and private information come through as a common thread in many writings on the topic of privacy (Solove, 2004, 2008; Moore, 2016; Tavani, 2008; Mayer-Schönberger, 2009; van Dijck, 2013; Mason, Mason, and Culnan, 1995), and as Weinberger (2007, p. 106) believes "put simply, the owners of information no longer own the organization of that information" once content takes on new life in an open environment. We live in a world of constant (almost endless) information sharing (Akpojivi, 2017, p. 271), where private information is frequently given, and documented, within many contexts as part of daily transactions. Perhaps it is human nature that individuals may not always read the terms of service or conditions for which we freely provide private information, or are not aware of how this information may be used (and reused) by outside entities.

A desire and attainment of privacy has been intensified and complicated within the world of connected resources and networks. It is increasingly difficult, perhaps nearly impossible, in the modern era to have an offline existence in the complete sense, without some discoverable, traceable digital tracks. Recently, there is an increased awareness of how information is used, retained, and transmitted and how to "opt-out" (when possible) of data collection and publication avenues, oftentimes after major privacy breaches or violations (such as the Cambridge Analytica/Facebook breach). There is often a conflict within the discussions of privacy as to whether this should be an inherent, baseline right for all, or if privacy is desired for purposes of concealment or secrecy. And as Warren and Brandeis wrote in their seminal work (1890) in the *Harvard Law Review*, entitled "The Right to Privacy," this concept could be referred to as the "right to be let alone" rather than a right to privacy. Should an individual assume a right of privacy as a default condition, or is this even possible in today's context?

As discussed above, privacy is a hotly contested term without an agreed consensus, and many scholars have resisted using a definitive meaning when using the term, and for good reason. Parent discussed the inconsistencies, ambiguities, and paradoxes that often revolve around the definition of privacy (Parent, 1983, p. 269). He went on to say that this aspect of privacy has led to the preclusion of society talking about privacy issues in a clear, effective manner. Vaidhyanathan equates the problem of privacy essentially circles around the issue of control by the individual, who has their own internal working definition:

> *Privacy is not just about personal choices, or some group of traits or behaviors we call "private" things. Nor are privacy concerns the same for every context in which we live and move. Privacy is an unfortunate term, because it carries with it no sense of its own customizability and contingency. When we complain about infringements of privacy, what we really demand is some measure of control over our reputations. Who should have the power to collection, cross-reference, publicize, or share information about us?* (Vaidhyanathan, 2011, p. 93).

In the book chapter entitled "Privacy, Freedom of Expression, and the Right to Be Forgotten," authors Kulk and Borgesius (2018) use the terms "privacy" and "private life" interchangeably. This is an interesting way to frame a conversation, as both as a notion of one's private life (more tangible) and as a more holistic conceptual term of privacy (less tangible). Likewise, Introna (1997, p. 262) talks about the notion of the "personal realm," and the inherent difficulty in defining what constitutes as both as something that is private or personal. Introna continues: "There is no ontologically defined personal realm," contrasting one example of an situation that may be considered quite private in one culture that is public in another. Intriguingly, Introna also poses the concept of privacy as something that is relational and relative within society as a continuum, and ultimately a matter of judgment (which begs the question, by whom?).

Kulk and Borgesius (2018) go on to state that under the European Court of Human Rights, privacy has also not been purposely defined extensively or precisely. Instead, it must be considered under the microscope of present-day conditions, or a living instrument doctrine, as opposed to finite definitions that may prove to be too limiting or restrictive. Further, the authors state that privacy and the freedom of expression have equal weight under current European courts, which consider the circumstances of the particular case as to which right will have more regard in the final decision, where some have pointed that the U.S. has sided more with the freedom of speech and expression.

Information, and access to information, is ultimately power, in its potential use, or misuse. And within the world where there is an almost perfect network of memory, content, and access in the shape of readily available digital information of all kinds, how can one escape without a certain level of private information being online? Depending on where one resides, a certain amount of information is readily available in free databases within public records can provide a huge amount of information on an individual, and make it increasingly difficult to lead an offline existence without some kind of digital identity. In the U.S., we have not come to a point to clearly define all of the variable definitions of privacy in law to date, whereas the EU has made further advancements in this area through protective laws.

But, we cannot (or perhaps should not) live by absolutes on either end (here I mean, absolute privacy vs. absolute exposure). As van den Herik and de Laa reflect (2016, p. 51), "the main point we make is that a total protection of privacy is impossible (and maybe even undesirable)," and so we find ourselves existing somewhere in the middle of the two extremes. As a collective, we need to better define a basic set of conditions for an agreed upon level of what a sufficient privacy level is for digital collections and begin to more clearly and readily identify working guidelines around privacy for practitioners. We can start this work in an attempt to solidify the elements found under existing laws such as HIPPA and FERPA here in the U.S. Add to this some of the other categories discussed above (and socially agreed upon) from the Tavani and Young charts. This process is fraught with issues in defining some baseline targets and potential biases, which will also need its own framework of checks and balances to ensure it is both reflective of the society and continuously updated at regular intervals. Such guidelines, however, would be most useful for practitioners to have on hand at the onset of new projects.

## 1.8    A DISCORD BETWEEN "INFORMATION (ALMOST) WANTS TO BE FREE" AND "NOT ALL INFORMATION WANTS TO BE FREE"

*Everywhere we remain unfree and chained to technology, whether we passionately affirm or deny it. But we are delivered over to it in the worst possible way when we regard it as something neutral; for this conception of it, to which today we particularly like to pay homage, makes us utterly blind to the essence of technology* (Heidegger, 1954, p. 311-312).

Recently, I had a discussion with Kent State colleague Dr. Michael Kavulic, who at the time had the title of Director of Board Operations and Technology, on the topic of digitizing the Board of Trustee meeting minutes and books. During this conversation, we talked through many details present in the particular digital project. This included the complexities of versioning between the copy present in the Office of the President and the (possibly different) copy in the University Archives holdings, the presence of known personally identifiable information in some board books, and occurrence of marginalia in some copies (which could contain private information by unknown authors), among other issues in setting up the project parameters. The board books, for example, sometimes contained personnel actions that included an employee's name, social security number, and salary. Kent State is a public state institution, and information on salary, for example, is available through other avenues of discovery in both analog and online resources. However, social security numbers were one element we agreed would be flagged for redaction before disseminating online, and was as such noted in the project parameters as a main privacy concern.

During this conversation, Dr. Kavulic made a comment to the effect of "not all information is created equal," and this idea has been stewing around in my mind ever since (and in my mind, this conflicted with Stewart Brand's aphorism "information wants to be free"[5] that I have in some sense been roughly abiding to throughout my professional career). I believe my colleague's comment was framed from the viewpoint that some information contained in the books should be restricted for privacy concerns and ultimately concealed in the public version (such as social security numbers), while other information is routinely shared without hesitation. The comment also considered the original intent of the creator, as well as the implications of time and place that are not the same factors present when we look to transmit this information more broadly.[6]

Perhaps until this point I had been fortunate to work mainly on projects that were either free and clear in terms of copyright and privacy, or the collections were adjoined with very specific, definitive permissions, documentation, donor agreements, or releases from content creators. Dr. Kavulics' comment led me to this particular line of inquiry in the examination of private information in digital collections, and most especially to think about the role of the practitioner takes in the project planning, selection, ultimate decision making, and eventual publication of such information. I have been especially grateful for the comment at that particular moment in time, since this is part of the underlying issue at the heart of the discussion presented here; when we, as practitioners, start to weigh various elements and make decisions about what constitutes as private information that should not be shared broadly online, there is an inherent inequality as a result.

---

[5]    Or is it that it "almost" wants to be free? I was intrigued to hear video footage of Brand's original quote had been unearthed only to discover he had been misquoted all these years: https://digitopoly.org/2015/10/25/information-wants-to-be-free-the-history-of-that-quote/.

[6]    Interesting discussion in Steven Bingo's (2011, p. 518) article on contextual integrity, and documents with "privileged access": of personal information, calling this situation third-party privacy. One example highlights this aspect perfectly, within a collection of letters between a travel writer and individuals who readily provided sensitive information within the context of written correspondence destined for one individual. Some letters were confessional in nature, and any disclosure of information beyond this scope had the potential to cause harm to the content producers.

While weighing the harm that could come from publishing personal identification numbers of living persons, there is a decision to remove/hide/conceal a piece of information from the original that is done so for the protection of others and to prevent potential harm. The example of social security numbers in the scenario above is a fairly straightforward one, since identity theft and other crimes often use these crucial pieces of private information to cause malice. While other aspects, like the handwritten marginalia that may trace a thought, comment, or other notion from an un-identified board member or administrator, who would likely not have anticipated the scribbled note would make it into a more permanent, global arena of discovery and access (and depending on the nature of the note, this disclosure online could create a liability if there was something written that may lead to further debate or argument if found to be problematic).

In Heidegger's scope of technology as we defined in the previous section, the element that has the potential to cause either good or malice is ultimately the human element, as the active agent. Technology is but a tool, brought to fruition by man and purposed to meet our specific needs and wants. By this thought, the information contained in digital collections is interpreted through technology by way of the associated tools and underlying technical infrastructure(s)—from the hardware and software that thrusts the information along the channels to be disseminated, in-terpreted and presented within a series of constructed, interconnected banks of storage containers that provides direct, immediate access. The active agent pushing the information to the point of "freedom" from its analog shell is man, with technology acting as the enabling piece in the equation to push information to be broadcast to an unlimited, worldwide audience. Further, Heidegger's notion of concealment and unconcealment resonated here in the process of freeing information through online dissemination, or conversely hiding information in decisions to redact or conceal, as decided by the project team. These conversations around privacy at the onset of the project are im-portant to create a higher degree of mindfulness and awareness around potential privacy violations. Information is transformed by the act of digital publication and transmission of the analog context from its analog form, and by pushing content into an open platform (or, in the case of born-digital, just the last step).

Let us look at an example of a private handwritten diary. The original context and inten-tion may be of the most private nature in the original context: a physical, material object that is concealed, and only known by its creator. This diary at a later date is deemed to be of interest for research, perhaps after the person dies. The diary is later digitized, transcribed, and uploaded to a digital collection. Now, the information contained cover to cover can be searched and discov-ered easily by anyone with the means to access the digital version. Each private scribbling is now elevated into an entirely different scope and arena, in moving the previously offline, closed infor-mation to a limitless, open access point. Gilliland and Wiener (2014) also cite the diary example to be particularly problematic, in that there could be damaging or embarrassing information that was not intended for public consumption. The authors call for an analysis of how the creator(s) (as well as those who may be impacted) intended the information to be consumed (p. 22), in defining the audience.

We could contrast this with the notion of a published book, which from its publication point was destined for the public sphere with the knowledge and awareness of broad dissemination. In the diary example, perhaps it is agreed upon by committee or working group the aspect that any privacy issues would be void after the individual's death, or that the research value outweighed the potential privacy violations of the original context.[7]

This notion of an item in the private vs. public sphere is an interesting one to ponder, as one may have disclosed very different information between the two. "Individuals reveal and guard private information differently depending on whether they are interacting with an intimate partner, a close friend, a casual acquaintance, or a coworker" (Davisson, 2016, p. 46). Ideas of permission and consent circle around the notion of context, which may or may not be easily ascertained within the parameters a project or available documentation on a potential item or collection.

The selection and scope of projects should always have a review of private information, which could be part of a checklist or workflow to address in the same light that other technical considerations or copyright concerns may be addressed. Presently in larger mass digitization digital projects that may focus on a large archival collection with minimal processing, privacy issues may have been overlooked in the interest of time or the lack of staffing to fully and more comprehensively address these concerns. Some institutions may also choose a riskier route of posting potentially damaging information, with the thought that items or certain information can be requested to be removed at a later date by way of a takedown request and removal. However, practitioners are overdue to act more deliberately, and consciously, around the potential of harm when publishing private data.

---

[7] There are some interesting exceptions within HIPPA regarding privacy violations, only in the more extreme circumstances of proving public interest or defining a benefit that would override or justify such an act of disclosure.

CHAPTER 2

# Core Ethical Theories and Decision making Frameworks

*Since I am a creature with a personal point of view, who has personal reasons, a morality that required me to transcend that point of view and think of the world as if I had no particular place in it would not merely be unreasonably demanding, it would deny all moral significance to the fact that my life is, in a sense, all I have. There has, therefore, to be some balance between the demands that the needs of others put on us and our right to live our own lives* (McNaughton and Rawling, 2006, p. 447).

## 2.1 BACKGROUND

This chapter briefly outlines two selected ethical theories for one to consider within the framework of ethical decision making. The purpose will be more cursory in nature, as to illustrate the core fundamentals of each theory and demonstrate how these can be applied broadly in practice for digital librarians. Ethics serves as a branch of moral philosophy, and is centered around the greater questions of right and wrong, good and evil, and all the gray areas that exist in between.

The function of ethics exists abstractly within a society, and as such, can adapt over time. Mills (1869) wrote that as individuals, a person lives within a particular society and the outlying framework that ultimately has the moral jurisdiction over one's affairs and conducts in the social world. An individual's society is always in motion, ever-adaptive in its definition and practice over time. As such, the approach in ethical decision making can also transform over time, making it difficult to solidify or set any definitive models with any amount of certainty. What is important for our purpose here is to become more aware and conscious of our personal biases that can impact decision making, and could also be in conflict with other ideologies existant at the institution or profession (if these have been defined elsewhere). With such diverse outlooks on the notion of privacy, this is a particularly slippery slope to navigate. Without a solid Code of Ethics in place to address some of these concerns, practitioners are often left to their own accord to act on trickier situations.

## 2.2 CONSEQUENTIALISM

Consequentialism is focused solely around the evaluation and consideration of potential consequence, both good and bad. Under this framework, actions can be examined in advance and reflected on as to the conceivable results, as far as those may be known in some scenarios. Benefit and harm are weighed and applied equally to all under this context in general, with decisions weighing toward the option to give the individual the greatest benefit and as much as possible, elude any harm.

Consequences can be deemed to be both direct and indirect to the individual, from the most dire and life-threatening to the more minor offenses. There are many interesting viewpoints within consequentialism as to how one consistently assesses and considers the value of harm and how one's outlook can impact on others (particularly if factors of any known bias is detected). For our purpose here, however, we will focus on the larger, perhaps more simplistic, concept of gauging harm through preventative appraisal of privacy violations within a project.

One of the more thought-provoking aspects of consequentialism is in the examination and consideration of probable consequences before the actual consequence is known. As outlined earlier, the potential of harm can be identified in the disclosure of information when placed into a larger network of connectivity and access. If we can isolate privacy concerns, the potential for harm comes directly in the disclosure of personal data, regardless of whether or not this harm is intentional or not (as Solove pointed out, privacy can be infringed upon even if no breach in private data). And as Hooker (2010, p. 451) writes, this analysis can be done within a quantifiable method and a value placed on each identified outcome, but also notes that "Real life is rarely so simple. Still, understanding often starts with the simplest cases."

Hooker goes on to discuss reasons why this consideration of consequence may not be occurring, with some reasons being: a lack of necessary information to make a decision; a lack of time; and difficulty assessing consequences and human limitations or biases. The lack of time may be the most likely reason that many practitioners have not gone through a more comprehensive, thorough review with an ethical framework. Assessing and identifying potential consequences is labor intensive and also prone to bias, and would take place after another time-consuming task, in the identification (and possible redaction) of personal data (Gilliland and Wiener, 2014).

## 2.3    DEONTOLOGICAL

Deontology is also an appealing theory to apply to ethical decision making in digital collections in that it represents a forward-thinking approach rather than one that favors the greater good. In deontology, overarching rules are used to determine right from wrong, wherein the morality of an action is judged on the action itself under the defined rules, and not focused on the latter consequences of the action. This greater good may not always be the more ethical stance, allowing for some scenarios to weigh the greater outcome (say, a conscious lie that prevents a murder). There are basic notions for deontologists that border on absolutes, i.e., one should not lie, murder innocent people, or torture other people (McNaughton and Rawling, 2006, p. 425). One crucial drawback in this ideology that Wood elaborated on is the overarching principle that all rules will be followed by all individuals (Wood, 2001). In many cases there may be more conditional, possibly individualistic, aspects of the scenario that could lead ultimately to exceptions to the rules within an institution, and between different individual viewpoints.

Deontology is an interesting application since acknowledgment situations are often not simply (or purely) "good" or "bad," giving consideration to the often grayer areas of life. This notion also accommodates for the difference in how individuals differ in how they view the world. Generally speaking, there is often an assumption of an individual's personal responsibility to do good in society (with many exceptions here, which I hesitate to generalize), although one's definition of how "good" can be accomplished and defined can vary greatly between individuals. These definitions of a personal responsibility vary greatly within a society, and throughout different cultures and the individual (Moore, 2016; Mills, 1869).

Examples to exceptions to contesting a wrong to make a right can be found in the cases of Chealsea Manning (WikiLeaks) and Edward Snowden (National Security Agency leaked documents), by way of the conflict of the overarching "good" by way of breaking a societal rule in their actions. The actions themselves can be deemed either right or wrong under deontology, although they can be contested in their holistic ethical implication in the resulting consequence (DeWolf, 1989). Akpojivi also reflects on the balance of factors when individuals consider an issue:

> Societies have increasingly different roles including safety, economic growth, political and cultural development, which they must play at different times. In the process of carrying out these roles, the privacy of individuals may be breached or individuals may have to forgo some of their privacy, hence the question of how ethical is it for institutions within society to pry into the activities of individuals without their knowledge. This question is salient as the revelations from Assange and Snowden highlight how nations could abuse their powers in the process of carrying out their moral jurisdictions, by simply generating digital dossier of the public, which doesn't necessarily help in the fight against terrorism (Akpojivi, 2017, p. 272).

These lines between the moral and immoral decisions may at times be quite difficult to discern, particularly when weighing contrasting values.

Deontology can be quite useful in defining the causal relationship, and personal reflections, within privacy and online content. We have already discussed the difficulties in pinpointing what privacy entails, and what constitutes private information. This difficulty has caused a scenario for practitioners who may have different connotations of what privacy means to them, and as such, how this is reflected directly within the workplace and subsequent decision making in digital projects.

## 2.4   ETHICAL DECISION MAKING: MODELS AND RESOURCES

*A dilemma or ethical issue often involves being caught between a rock and a hard place, a situation involving a choice between equally unsatisfactory alternatives* (Wood, 2001, p. 10).

Ethical decision making can result in the necessity of making exceedingly challenging decisions, very often with few clear indications as to discerning the underlying right or wrong of the matter. There may very well be situations where a committee and working group do not see eye to eye or are able to come to a consensus in particularly dubious examples. The eventual resolutions of ethical dilemmas may have guidance from professional standards, codes of ethics, or other locally defined institutional policies in place. And when a group of professionals is lacking a Code of Ethics to offer guidance, it can be difficult to find solid principles or core values to help practitioners in day-to-day ethical conundrums. Although in the absence of such written documentation it will be imperative that the individuals charged with decision making be held accountable in some way after a final decision is made, keeping in mind core ethical theories as a baseline in decision making.

A useful resource that can be used broadly in any situation is the Curtin 6-step model (Curtin, 1978) for breaking down the steps in ethical decision making, which outlines the following:

1. perception of the problem;

2. identification of ethical components;

3. clarification of persons involved;

4. exploration of options;

5. application of ethical theory; and

6. resolution/evaluation.

This model outlines a process that is indicative of an information gathering process, at the very onset of a privacy review. The model also has points of discussion and reflection, which could be incredibly useful for working groups and committees to consider and use as a starting point once private information has been identified.

Two of the steps in particular outlined in Curtin's model are of special interest in the digital library landscape. In the second step, there is an analysis to identify the problematic areas and also work to define the individuals who are affected by the dilemma, such as the presence of private data in our scenario. Particularly within a group setting, there may be varying vantage points and opinions between individuals as to what the ethical components ultimately are, although this is a valuable step to defining an issue collectively (like within a working group). The third step is also an important one to highlight as the process seeks to identify the impacted person(s), and also define the rights that they may be allowed in the scenario. Curtin's model can certainly be applied locally while initiating a new project, at any scale, as a useful tool to work into conversations around defining potential problems.

Similarly, Linda Klebe Trevino looked at ethical decision making within an organization, using situational variables to explain behaviors. The author stated that ethical issues are most in conflict in uncertain conditions that involve many individuals, interests, and values (Trevino, 1986, p. 601). The author also discussed the idea that an individual's personal ethical standards are used a default *when no organizational ones are present*. Further, the underlying moral behaviors of the individual was often at the crux of decision making in Trevino's examples, where the scenario is directly impacted by the specific viewpoint of the individual.

Trevino also speculates that the frequency at which one is required to make resolutions of moral conflicts aligns directly to the level of cognitive moral development (i.e., the more frequent we have to test ethically murky waters, perhaps the more comfortable we are in our overall decision making). Take, for instance, an emergency room nurse who makes daily decisions that directly impact the course of treatment of dying patients, as compared to the collection manager who may rarely receive questions or be in dilemmas that push at ethical consideration outside of the normal day-to-day routine. When pressured to make frequent decisions with ethical considerations, one would likely be more readily versed to test their internal moral compass for guidance.

Trevino also considers the role of consequence and responsibility of the individual, which are often molded institutionally by authoritative figures. The author further discusses the presence and role of guiding documents or a code of ethics, which in some cases may not be more than "window dressing" and ultimately ineffective (Trevino, 1986, p. 613), unless there is strong support and understanding of the documents. Codes of ethics are also not legally binding, but instead serve as a framework or an agreed ideology for a defined group of people to share and morally abide to follow. Finally, the author finds that "the most ethical behavior was achieved under the condition where unethical behavior was clearly punished" (Trevino, 1986, p. 614).

In another example from the nursing context, DeWolf (1989) writes about the process at which a nurse resolves ethical scenarios as part of daily job expectations. The decision making process for a nurse likely occurs under a very different duress of time and immediacy of life and death that other professions would not necessarily endure as intensely. She writes about the role of the nurse to be an advocate for the patient, which we could likewise draw parallels with the library scenario as the practitioner is the voice and ultimate caretaker of the library patron, subject, and end user. In this light, we can remind ourselves to first consider the individual who could be impacted directly as result of the decision to broadly share potentially private information. DeWolf also addresses known conflicts that can arise within the belief system of an individual, which can serve as an obstacle for the individual in making a choice between two competing principles (one more extreme example provided of a decision where an individual has a personal and ethical conflict that exists between abortion and the right to life).

DeWolf also advocates for the use of decision trees, a more schematic way to provide an outline of both process and decision making. The creation of a decision tree can anticipate potential problems and act as an aid in project management at all levels. Concisely created decision trees can provide an easy reference for anyone working on a project to flag potential issues, and serve as a place to outline and anticipate some obstacles. For example, an institution may have to decide on a list of agreed upon articles of what constitutes personal data not to be shared broadly, and provide that within a decision tree as an action point; say, social security numbers, student identification numbers, grades, health information, driver license numbers, and any financial information are deemed to be an immediate flag for review or redaction, while information around more ambiguous personal details such as address, age, or other may be separated for review by a project manager or working group.

DeWolf further breaks down consequence into three areas: the foreseeable, the actual/known, or the possible. She also acknowledges that oftentimes decision making can take place without an individual fully considering the real-world ramification of the decision, particularly with the regard to the aspect of risk. There needs to be a place for this consideration and discussion to be more at the forefront of project proposals to adequately address the notion of consequence as result of openly publishing content online. In the same way many institutions may view copyright as a potential risk within digital projects, practitioners need to accept responsibility for their role in pushing concealed information into open arenas of discovery.

In DeWolf's article, the author outlines four elements that occur during ethical decision making, similar to Curtin's (1989, p. 79) model:

1. identify all possible options;

2. identify the outcomes associated with each option;

3. identify the probability that the option will produce the desired result(s); and

4. identify the importance the decision-maker ascribes to each possible option.

The fourth element addresses the differences that the decision-maker as an individual holding specific beliefs may bring into the situation. With regard to defining privacy, this can be extremely problematic, as we have noted that the individual reflection of what constitutes privacy can differ greatly between individuals. What one practitioner may consider a private piece of information that is not approppriate for public consumption, another may not, further necessitating the use of decision trees or other agreed upon documentation to assist in the identification and decision making processes. Lastly, DeWolf calls for a mechanism for feedback throughout the ethical decision making, and also for an integration of an ethical awareness to be present at employee training and onboarding, as well as continual development opportunities to further allow the individual to develop beneficial decision making skill sets (1989, p. 80).

Finally, one last article that resonated and echoed the idea of a personal level of investment and considering the variable of the individual's beliefs and viewpoints was in Ruedy and Schweitzer's article on the idea of mindfulness in ethical decision making. The author outlined the need for an increased level of awareness by the individual throughout the decision making process. The authors completed a study that found the more mindful the decision maker, the more ethical the result was. "Mindful individuals may feel less compelled to ignore, explain away, or rationalize ideas that might be potentially threatening to the self, such as a conflict of interest or potential bias." (Ruedy and Schweitzer, 2010, p. 76). This aspect of mindfulness is especially relevant to the second and third case studies.

One case study focused on ethical decision making examined the role of awareness and mindfulness, where individuals were placed in front of a mirror. This awareness of self led to less cheating in a study done in 1976 by Diener and Wallbom, as mentioned in the Ruedy and Schweitzer article. The authors also found that the *smaller the perception* of the ethical infraction, the more likely the individual was to make the unethical decision. The definition of both small and large consequences of action is essential to convey in the mindful decision-maker, moving toward a self-calibrated, mindful moral compass is crucial to the success of the ethical librarian, who can make detections of ethical infractions both small and large.

However, the awareness of what constitutes an ethical conundrum can certainly differ between individuals, who may have varying thresholds of what would constitute as a violation. Yet, Ruedy and Schweitzer believe that an increase in the mindfulness in tasks both large and small will ultimately lead to more ethical decisions by the individual. If practitioners worked Curtin or DeWolf's models into project planning, this would inevitably create a more mindful process overall, and create a process in which we begin to recognize potential ethical infringements, as recommended in the Appendix.

In addition to the idea of defining consequence, Ruedy and Schweitzer also talk about the notion of surveillance within the decision making system (i.e., someone who has an awareness of being observed will often make more ethical decisions than someone in a scenario with little to no surveillance). Increased discussion on the notion of accountability and documentation of decision making in the process is an area for further research, although on this topic if we take some initial steps of creating decision trees and referring to models such as Curtin or DeWolf as described above we will make a move toward progress.

## 2.5    EXAMPLES OF CODE OF ETHICS

*We need to question how we can devise a mediated ethics which attempts to counteract the more alienating and objectifying aspects of non-proximal, mediated encounters with others. At the same time, if we are able to retain any sense of privacy or autonomy in a world of increasing commercial data collection, we also need to recognise the nature of contemporary selves and their non-material existence in digital technologies as dispersed, parallel assemblages and thus consider expanding the notion of "self", legally and in ethical practice, to include the presences we achieve through technology—not only the self-conscious ones of avatars and profiles but also the databases, images* and all other forms of data extracted from us (Miller, 2016, p. 114, my emphasis).

The ALA's Code of Ethics mentions privacy within a different framework in part 3: "We protect each library user's right to privacy and confidentiality with respect to information sought or received and resources consulted, borrowed, acquired or transmitted" (American Library Association, 2008). This more directly addresses patron behavior, and not so much as the privacy concerns that are illustrated above. An update to ALA's code reflects other types of private information contained elsewhere in the library or library collections as responsible gatekeepers. Librarian Dorothea Salo has also recommended adding the following privacy concerns: "Privacy of research subjects in collected data, privacy of living individuals mentioned in archival materials, privacy of confidential business records and privacy for especially vulnerable individuals" (Salo, 2013, slide 3).

Moreover, we can also look to the "Access and Use" section of the Society of American Archivists (SAA) who has a Code of Ethics addressing privacy in the following.

*Archivists formulate and disseminate institutional access policies along with strategies that encourage responsible use. They work with donors and originating agencies to ensure that any restrictions are appropriate, well-documented, and equitably enforced. When repositories require restrictions to protect confidential and proprietary information, such restrictions should be implemented in an impartial manner. In all questions of access, archivists seek practical solutions that balance competing principles and interests* (SAA Code of Ethics, 2012).

Archivists have long dealt with balancing access with privacy concerns for decades within their collections. Depending on the archive, there may be differing policies and practices in place to address this tension (Bingo, 2011). Benedict reflects that archivists work in a space that often weighs three main considerations in the course of a regular day: the privacy of the individual, the policy(ies) of the institution, and the researcher's right to information (Benedict, 2003, p. 18).

The International Federations of Library Associations and Institutions (IFLA) has a Code of Ethics with a notable section on privacy, secrecy, and transparency. The first line reads; "Librarians and other information workers respect personal privacy, and the protection of personal data, necessarily shared between individuals and institutions" (IFLA, Section 3), yet in the same section it stresses the importance of supporting transparency particularly around government, administration, and business to the general public. Here, the audience is loosely defined; protect the personal information of the individual user, although other entities are to be held to different standards.

The Association of Computing Machinery (ACM) highlight privacy in their Code of Ethics, under a clause 1.7, entitled, "Respect the privacy of others."

> *This imperative implies that only the necessary amount of personal information be collected in a system, that retention and disposal periods for that information be clearly defined and enforced, and that personal information gathered for a specific purpose not be used for other purposes without consent of the individual(s)* (ACM Code of Ethics, 1992).

The idea of a "necessary amount of personal information" is interesting to consider, particularly if it is deemed irrelevant, as one of the factors in the Right to be Forgotten. And, they also touch on the idea of gaining consent if there is a different notion outside of the original purpose to use the information.

Another interesting example to look at is the discussion of using publicly shared information from social media accounts within research and adjoining publications. There has been a noted disagreement in the arena of gaining consent for the use of publicly available social media content among researchers (Haimson, Andalibi, Pater, 2016), and whether researchers should act to alert individuals to the use through either an opt-in or opt-out approach. The authors discuss their approach in a recent publication, where they contacted 17 individuals directly through the social media messaging system. They gave a set amount of time (five months) for individuals to respond. They further removed any identifiable features in their publication (profile pictures, username, etc.), and in the end received responses from 3 of the 17 accounts. The other individuals very well may not be aware of the use of their social media data, but from the viewpoint of the researchers, due diligence was done. "Apparently, it is easier to encode sociality into algorithms than to decode algorithms back into social actions" (van Dijck, 2013, p. 172).

In this last example, there was also discussion about whether or not using publicly available social media qualifies as being a participant or not, since there is not an awareness in place that there would be under normal, institutional review board (IRB) approved research surveys and interviews. Additionally, the topic of harm vs. benefit is used here, as to whether or not the overall study and use of this data is appropriate. This case differs from much of what we have talked about here, since this information was already public, although there is the parallel that it is the *context* that has changed here; "…the researcher fundamentally changes the presentation and the meaning of the post" (Haimson, Andalibi, Pater, 2016, p. 2). Private information has been repackaged and reused for a different purpose of the original setting, and another important element is that the *control* has been shifted by this use. For example, if the data used in the original study, which is focused on eating disorders, is published in an anonymized form, there are traces that can lead a reader back to the origins, essentially outing the original author in a context that was not in their control.

Finally, in the article "Ten Simple Rules for Responsible Big Data Research," the authors outline many of the issues we have discussed throughout this title, such as context and consequence. The second rule states "recognize that privacy is more than a binary issue," and reiterates the notion of the impact of decisions and actions on others that could potentially bring harm by use of information. The authors also recommend developing a code of conduct within your respective community around practice, ethical data sharing, and the notion of auditability.

## 2.6    CONCLUSION

> *The purpose of the societal moral compass map is to arrive at an informed judgment as to the balance to be struck between opposing poles in forming a good and ethical society* (Mason, Mason, Culnan, 1995, p. 248).

Finding the balance and making an informed judgment is the goal of ethical decision making; in creating more deliberate, thoughtful reflections we think more holistically about privacy issues and ramifications within published online content. Another aspect to consider as we move into the next chapter on the topic of ethics, which is heavily inspired by the "Ethical decision making and Internet research" recommendations from the Association of Internet Researchers (AoIR) ethics working committee in 2012. In the recommendations, there is a decision to take on an "ethical pluralism." This concept addresses the concept of ethical conflict between ideologies that can arise from using different ethical frameworks. That is to say, what might be deemed as the more ethical choice under one framework may be found less ethical under a different rationale. The AoIR working committee further notes that due to the nature of the World Wide Web, we must also consider the diverse cultural viewpoints as being a universal resource, and in many cases use a blended model to best make ethical decisions to reflect differing belief systems. Likewise, digital collections are often served to a worldwide network, increasing potential conundrums and issues in ethical decision making.

Practitioners can use and refer to the specific ethical frameworks present in consequentialism and deontology to aid in decision making, and we may, in the end, find ourselves creating a composite of these theories using selected values and elements. These frameworks cannot serve as absolutes, and will need to adapt to changes in society and culture over time. Privacy issues complicate matters since these are also difficult to pinpoint and define, however an increased mindfulness overall and thus be a move in the profession to create more systematic review points will help address problems more uniformly.

As van der Sloot notes, we are always within a sea of change:

> *The commonality between these theories is precisely that privacy is directed at curtailing and limiting norms. This might explain why the meaning and value of privacy seems to be a chameleon; it is not privacy that keeps on transforming, it is the norms that do so* (van der Sloot, 2016, p. 124).

As such, our constructed frameworks will need to have an area for review and updates in this shifting landscape. Gilliland and Wiener (2014) outline a process to create a privacy audit process, and recommend first consulting any specific institution policy and applicable state laws, as well as one's legal counsel during this process.

CHAPTER 3

# Role of the Practitioner as Active Agent and Notions of Privacy in Digital Collections

*This first element of folk morality—a deeply ingrained cultural and legal relativism-proves to be inadequate to address the new and unfamiliar moral and legal challenges arising in the cyber domain, where notions of "privacy" and "liberty" are often advanced as universal claims, demanding the respect of all citizens and governments* (Lucas, 2017, p. 36).

At a fundamental view, there is a physical state change when an item is digitized and then disseminated widely online. Information that was previously restricted in terms of access and discoverability by its analog container has been "freed" to a new, wider level of dissimination. This action has a consequence, for better or worse, of opening a portal or access point, particularly when there is the presence of a better quality OCR and full text indexing of the item in an openly accessible repository. Many of these consequences are positive ones. A scholar who might be searching for the title but is unable to travel to one of the holding libraries to access the content in person is now able to find a digital surrogate in a simple web search, and perhaps the digital form is also better primed for text analysis.[8] Or an analog reel-to-reel audio tape that was largely inaccessible within a special collection who may not have a method of playback even for on-site patrons and a minimal catalog description, which after digitization, is shared broadly and transcribed, pushing content from the concealed to the discoverable.

Conversely, there may well be negative aspects in this conversion and publication processes. Information that was previously difficult to find is now available at the end of a simple web search. For example, many institutions who have digitized a full-run of the student or local newspapers have often received takedown requests after online publication, as all the information contained in the historical issues is not always positive news for the individual, such as a campus police blotter section. The unconcealment of information (to use Heidegger's (1954) notion of unconcealment) through broad dissemination can unintentionally provide access to previously hidden or confidential content. These consequences may not be immediately apparent at the onset of the project, but

---

[8]  Interesting work on text analysis that has come from digital archives with comprehensive author editions. One example of this can be seen in the Willa Cather digital collections that have expounded on the potential of text analysis tools between editions of one author's work to highlight this concept. https://cather.unl.edu/.

by embedding a process to review and consider these elements, we can start to work this into project parameters at the beginning stage.

In *Everything is Miscellaneous* (2007, p. 104), Weinberger describes this process of moving from analog to digital as *increasing the leverage of knowledge*. The potential of access and being discovered comes primarily from the metadata records, and the higher chance of discoverability of the content in digital form, noting "Now that everything in the connected world can serve as metadata, knowledge is empowered beyond fathoming." This statement is intriguing since it gets at the idea that we cannot fully comprehend the use, value, and long-lasting impact of publishing content online, in both positive and negative aspects.

Reformatting analog material into a digital container and sharing broadly (or, the change of state, from offline to online) is where the role of the practitioner is most apparent in this process, but also perhaps under researched in terms of their accountability of any resulting harm or consequence. Practitioners effectively shepherd content from their analog containers to the digital, at times supplementing with the addition of full text searching or other aspects that deepen the potential for discoverability and access. It is our responsibility as a profession to be conscious, and more mindful, of the ramifications of this transition, and also determine some places where discussion on open access or redaction or other limitations would be in order. Mayer-Schönberger (2009, p. 52). states that four technological drivers have facilitated this transition to take place: in the combination of the digitization, cheap storage, easy retrieval, and global reach of information Add to this the growing digital repositories, and it becomes increasingly probable to expose private information.

While I do not suggest that we put the brakes on a project merely for the trickier privacy issues, I do think we need a more thoughtful, careful, and comprehensive review before publishing content. Practitioners need to be more conscious of the consequence(s) of publishing content to growing digital repositories, particularly with regard to personal data. It may not be immediately possible for smaller-staffed operations to add the extra step and required time for such consideration and granular review of privacy, although practitioners need to acknowledge the responsibility and become more culpable for the role we hold in these positions. Practitioners ultimately need to weigh the gravity of privacy concerns with that of open access, and also make decisions that best protect the content creator or subject of the private information.

## 3.1    ADDRESSING THE NOTION OF HARM

> *…Information begets information: as data is structured and analyzed it yields implications, consequences and predictions* (Nissenbaum, [2010], p. 37).

There is the ever-present potential of the misuse of data as a decontextualized entity, and a danger of misinterpretation and re-use for other purposes. The ability to pull together disparate information for potentially harmful purposes becomes easier as tools to collect information improve and the amount of information available increases. Mayer-Schönberger (2009, p. 110) states this information within open and connected networks can be "remembered" and recalled at any time. This scenario allows for information to be more readily accessible to an unlimited number of recipients "for vastly different purposes, while being perceived as undeniably precise and objective." While we may not be able to fully conceive of how any given item will be used in the future, we can take steps to take preventative measures to prevent the distribution of information that has the potential to damage or harm the individual.

The potential of harm can be found by way of publishing small, disparate pieces of information on an individual which is later used negatively against the same individual, either when combined together or used alone for other purposes.

> *Our digital presence, by its nature, is reduced to calculative bits in which the subjective meaning has been stripped away by technology itself. The link between the qualities of a person and the person itself has already been severed as the body of our digital existence is endlessly and ceaselessly abstracted and commodified through the endemic data collection technologies that continually monitor our net presence in various ways* (Miller, 2016, p. 67).

While the decision in the initial publication of information may have been oblivious as to the potential of harm, there needs to be an increased awareness and consideration made by the practitioner as to the adverse consequences. Curtin's and DeWolf's models can assist in identifying areas in which private information is present and therefore avoid harm.

## 3.2    THE RIGHT TO BE FORGOTTEN AND THE EU DATA PRIVACY LAWS

> *I never understood why when you died, you didn't just vanish, and everything could just keep going on the way it was only you just wouldn't be there. I always thought I'd like my own tombstone to be blank. No epitaph and no name. Well, actually, I'd like it to say "figment"* (Andy Warhol, 1985, p. 126–9).

I have long been intrigued with Andy Warhol. Not so much for the aesthetics of his stylized pop art, but more for his humor, quirky persona, and strange attempt at self-preservation through his largest serial artwork, the *Time Capsules*. Over the course of 13 years (ca. 1974–1987), Warhol filled nearly 600 cardboard boxes with odd assortments of material and objects from his everyday existence; photographs, newspapers, magazines, fan letters, dinner invitations, phone messages, and other ephemera such as movie ticket stubs or other daily random material traces.

It was an awareness on his part that these time capsules would eventually be sifted through, inventoried, conserved, considered, and valued at a minute level. Many years ago, I visited the Warhol Museum in Pittsburgh, Pennsylvania where there was a small exhibit that gave a glimpse of the utter randomness within the contents of one of the time capsules. One of the museum docents described some time capsules as being more purposefully selected than others. Some boxes were more chaotic and random, as if he simply dumped the contents of his desk into a box one afternoon, sealed the box tight and scratched the date on the side of the box.

On the day of my visit, there was an odd, eclectic assortment of items with no apparent relationship other than the date scribbled on the outside of the box. By creating these time capsules, Warhol assumed (correctly, I may add) that someone in the future would place value on these items and eventually churn through with painstaking attention to catalog and describe the contents of each time capsule. I have always thought of this work to be Warhol's joke from beyond the grave, perhaps knowing the hours of work it would take to sift through these boxes, particularly after reading about his other outrageous behavior and anecdotes over the course of his life.[9]

While looking through the digital collections from the Andy Warhol museum, it seems he also included items such as passports and other personal effects containing private information from his life. In this light, the quote above is more curious, considering Andy Warhol went to great lengths to self-immortalize his name and include many strange and random tidbits of his life through the *Time Capsules* work, and these are contrasted with his often quirky contradictory actions and statements.

There is ultimately a conflict between the desire for privacy and the action of encapsulating himself within the *Time Capsules*. (Or, does this point to a differing viewpoint within one's life on the subject? In that, perhaps he had one belief at one time, and had changed his outlook later in life over a desire to be forgotten in time? Or, perhaps Andy Warhol wanted to be a true enigma- His interviews were often filled with curious and sometimes contrary statements to add a level of perplexing complexity to the aura of his persona and work.) We can also return to the notion that one's desire for privacy ends after death (or the right to privacy).

I use the example of the *Time Capsules* as a situation where we may have conflicting information around a collection or even a person with regard to privacy, in that we have some statements from the individual that point to a desire of erasure, yet whose actions and work reflect a different ideology. How far does intent of the creator go in balancing the notion of individual privacy and digital dissemination? Mayer-Schönberger (2009, p. 103) reminds us about the idea of durability within the digital world: "Before digital memory most information, even incriminating items, were forgotten relatively quickly." Warhol spoke from the point of view of a different time within a purely analog world, one which gave anonymity by virtue of its inherent disconnect and not being able to quickly retrieve information, and likely could not have fathomed the future digital reality in which we now subsist.

---

[9]  A collection of some of Warhol's more curious and entertaining quotes can be found here: http://www.complex.com/style/2014/08/the-best-andy-warhol-quotes/being-smart-makes-you-depressed.

Marjolein Lanzig reflects on this notion of an all-encompassing, accessible digital archive.

*Finally, a more permanent digital archive will have a self-disciplining or Panoptic effect. Instead of experimenting and being creative in our actions and decisions, the fact that all will be saved and could come to haunt you at a later stage, during a job interview for instance, may actually petrify you. If digital forgetfulness or forgiveness does not exist, we will become afraid to make mistakes. After all, we cannot reconfigure these mistakes as part of a learning process and as part of our narrative identity, because the digital record mercilessly presents the "facts" and presents the verdict about "future you" on who you once were or what you once did* (Lanzig, 2016, p. 86).

To contrast this idea of the permanent digital artchive, the "Right to be Forgotten" is intriguing to apply as a confounding element in this conversation for practitioners to consider an individual's perspective and desire for erasure, or the notions of digital forgetfulness or forgiveness. In particular, Western societies have reflected on this idea of erasure very differently, particularly in the contrast between the U.S. and European ideologies.

As result of the 2014 "Right to be Forgotten" court case in the EU (*Google, Inc. v Agencia Española de Protección de Datos, Mario Costeja Gonzállez*), there is now a process[10] in place for European citizens to request the removal of personal information (his name) from search engine results to comply with overarching data privacy laws. In the original court case, the individual (Mario Costeja Gonzállez) desired the removal of information from an early 1990s digitized newspaper regarding the foreclosure of his home due to an unpaid debt, a debt he later repaid. The courts ultimately sided with the Plaintiff and ordered Google to remove the link to the article from any search result in the EU. The core European data privacy laws (namely, the Data Protection Directive (95/46/EC)) also helped support this decision from the court. This scenario is applicable to digital librarians with regard to the fact that these types of direct requests may come from individuals for removals and takedown of information in digital collections (and arguably more directly damaging to overall accessibility by tampering with the original digital item and adjoining metadata record, and not merely the search engine results as in the EU case). The desire from the perspective of the individual to have control over digital content referencing a piece of information that they feel is private is at the heart of the Right to be Forgotten.

As a result of the EU court case, the definition and characteristics of what qualifies for removal in Europe is also intriguing as the outlined framework in Google's Transparency Report. Identified data must be found to be "inadequate, irrelevant or no longer relevant, or excessive" (Google, 2014). Privacy and the desire for deletion, as seen in The Right to be Forgotten case in

---

[10] More information on this framework can be found on the *Google Transparency Report*, under Search removals under European privacy law, https://transparencyreport.google.com/eu-privacy/overview?hl=en. Accessed April 15, 2018.

Spain, have some potential crossovers in the rationale of individuals seeking removal of private information of published material online within digital collections.

As a whole, EU citizens have had a more defined, prominent and ultimately enforceable mandates and articles around the right to privacy and data protection (European Convention on Human Rights, Articles 8 and 10; Data Protection Directive; General Data Protection Regulation (GDPR), as well as the individual national laws). Interestingly, some of the directives also address both the subject *and* receiver of information. There is also a set of criteria that is used by courts to address the balance of privacy and freedom of expression in the following:

1. contribution to a debate of general interest;

2. how well known the person concerned is;

3. the subject of the report;

4. the prior conduct of the person concerned;

5. the method of obtaining the information and its veracity;

6. the content, form, and consequences of the publication; and

7. the severity of the sanction imposed.

As cited in paragraph no. 110, *Delfi v. Estonia*, 64569/09 (2015).

This list of criteria can assist practitioners in how we regard information and its context, and in trying to attain a balance between two conflicting notions of privacy and the right to access information.

As a contrast to this, the U.S. has often sided with the notion of free speech over the idea of the right to deletion or erasure, perhaps as a tenant in the American notion of a democratic society and the prominence of the First Amendment. And, as Amber Davvison (2016, p. 45) states, online as well, "Free and unrestricted speech is regarded as a necessity for the development of a truly democratic web." In the first case study, we will examine how a court case addressing a takedown request regarding information in a student digital newspaper collection was handled, a case not entirely too dissimilar from the Right to Be Forgotten court case in 2014.

In in the U.S., there are some private services being developed to replicat this type of framework available in the EU for individuals to request removal of information. One such company is Right2remove.us, who states:

> *None of this information should be searchable on search engines under an individual's name: mugshots, criminal records, revenge porn, harassment, sexuality, bullying, minors, hate speech, race, citizenship, religious beliefs, political affiliations, interpersonal relationships, health conditions, disabilities, drug use, financial status, personal identi-*

*fication. The Right to Remove adapts and improves the Right To Be Forgotten for the United States. The policy is designed to navigate freedom of speech and privacy laws. Beyond this campaign, it provides practical removal solutions through automated take-down scripts, legal advice, and support for the individuals affected* (Right2remove.us homepage, retrieved February 2, 2018).

Also of interest is the fact that the site also claims to serve as a platform for those who cannot afford legal or technical means to address their concerns. This includes online reputation management solutions, and for individuals under pressure from personal relationships, state apparatuses, and financial difficulties.

## 3.3    CONFLICT OF FREE SPEECH AND PRIVACY

In the U.S., there is an inherent conflict between one's right to privacy and the First Amendment. Privacy has often also clashed with other issues, such as concerns around national security and Freedom of Information Act (2009), which states "A democracy requires accountability, and accountability requires transparency." This notion of transparency through accessible information directly conflicts with one's right and expectation of privacy, particularly under the veil of national security in the post 9/11 landscape. This concept is also at the crux of the conundrum for practitioners, who may personally value notions of privacy or open access in different regards (or may just feel a constant strain between these two concepts).

There has historically been a lack of solid data privacy laws in the U.S., particularly when you consider the currently ones in place in the European Union and within its member countries for decades. The 1974 Privacy Act in the U.S. has been the fundamental statute for data protection, though this is certainly in need of updating when one considers the scope of the world in 1974 as compared to modern society. There are, however, some interesting points from the Privacy Act to highlight in our application here in three principles.

- **Disclosure principle:** There must be a way for a person to find out what information about the person is in a record and how it is used.

- **Secondary usage principle:** There must be a way for a person to prevent information about the person that was obtained for one purpose from being used or made available for other purposes without the person's consent.

- **Security principle:** Any organization creating, maintaining, using, or disseminating records of identifiable personal data must assure the reliability of the data for their intended use and must take precautions to prevent misuse of the data.

The Privacy Act of 1974, 5 U.S.C. § 552a.

The disclosure aspect can be seen in digital repositories in the unconcealment of information, or data that an individual may not have been aware of previously due to the analog state until published online and later disclosed. The secondary usage principle points to a need for an avenue of communication between the subject of the data, the individual, and the information disseminator, with regard to request removal or limitation of certain information. And, finally, the security aspect speaks to the validity of the information as a responsibility of the publisher and the awareness to prevent misuse. We will delve more into the ideas of control and context of information in the next chapter.

In these last two sections, we have referred primarily to the Western world, comparing the U.S. and the EU, in part to highlight this notion of varying cultural and societal viewpoints when it comes to privacy and individual rights even within similar cultural frameworks. We have not considered non-Western cultures as it relates to privacy, but researchers like Ricardo Punzalan, Sally Jo Cunningham, Masood Masoodian, and Anne Adams have begun exploring these lines of inquiry in very compelling ways on this topic. This is another interesting avenue for exploration, though is not included in the purview of this title. Next, we will look at three case studies and consider how the aspect of privacy in each scenario factored into the scenario.

## 3.4    REAL-WORLD EXAMPLES: LAWSUITS, CASE STUDIES, AND OTHER RELEVANT RESEARCH

Three case studies are included here that align with examining notions of privacy in digital collections, beginning with perhaps the most straightforward example, and working into the more complex. First, we will examine the case of a student newspaper digitization project within an academic institution, centered around the request for the removal of printed information from an analog print source. This particular selection is also one of the few examples of a digital collection that has been put into the courtroom and went to trial. Then, we will examine the example of the digitization of a full-run analog lesbian erotic publication by a non-profit company, and how social pressure to remove access to the title ensued due to privacy. Finally, we will look at a different kind of digital collection, in a socially constructed setting, outside of an institutionally managed setting, with an example of a selected subreddit.

**Case study #1: Cornell Student Newspaper Lawsuit**

In January 2009, a judge dismissed an appeal of a lawsuit involving a digital version of a 1983 Cornell student newspaper. Plaintiff Kevin Vanginderen, a Cornell alum, had filed two consecutive lawsuits against Cornell in October 2007 and April 2008 after discovering a news item in the digital archive which reported Mr. Vanginderen's 1983 charge for burglary.

The Plaintiff discovered the information when the print newspaper was published in digital form on an openly accessible digital platform (eCommons), which effectively created an easily searchable inlet to the full-text content of the newspaper. Court records state that a Google search of his own name in the Fall of 2007 provided the Plaintiff with access to the digital version of the analog material. The information itself had not changed between the analog and digital versions, but the avenue and ability of discovery had greatly enhanced access. The original container of the print media restricted dissemination to those who could physically access the newspaper and pore through its pages, and once the paper was digitized and indexed, it pushed the information into a new arena of access and use. However, the central element in this particular case as it went to trial was the notion of truth as supported by various court documents (particularly interesting when we contrast this case study with the similar case of the Right to be Forgotten Spanish court, who sided with the Plaintiff).

There were multiple incidents of petit larceny and burglaries over the course of a year, as shown in court records in the original charge against the Plaintiff, reportedly totaling up to $474 worth of stolen goods. The newspaper printed one paragraph outlining the final charge in March of 1983, in the *Cornell Chronicle* in the "Blotter Barton" column. In the first suit, Vanginderen, who also happened to be a practicing lawyer in California at the time of the lawsuits, asserted libel and public disclosure of private facts by way of the digital version of the student newspaper.

Vanginderen initially claimed that the information in the Cornell Chronicle was not true, and led to loss of reputation and mental anguish. The court found evidence from city and county court records to support the facts contained in the digital news item, and further felt that the "Plaintiff had failed to establish that he would prevail on his claims because the gist of the Cornell Chronicle article *was true*" (Vanginderen v. Cornell, 2009, my emphasis) and granted Cornell's motion to strike the complaint. Vanginderen then filed a second suit against Cornell University and their attorney for libel, false light, public disclosure of private fact, and intrusion into private affairs, since previously sealed court records of Mr. Vanginderen's criminal history were included in court briefs and motions in the first complaint.

When Vanginderen initiated the second lawsuit in April 2008, the lawsuit and adjoining news coverage on the cases would effectively bring even more attention to the matter, akin to the "Streisand Effect" where the effort of trying to disclose or hide something has the opposite effect ("What is the Streisand Effect?", 2013). With this in mind, the notion of privacy is therefore further strained by way of the lawsuit following its natural course and has brought more attention and awareness to the original news item, an aspect that this particular Plaintiff would have been well aware of in his position as a practicing lawyer.

Information about this case was both present in city and county records from two rounds of charges, although the county records were sealed until the time Mr. Vanginderen filed his first lawsuit in 2007. The Plaintiff further purported that the unsealing and filing of the original court documents as a result of the lawsuit further pressed the issue of privacy from the point of view of the Plaintiff who also alleged that Cornell knew that these documents would then be distributed more broadly online via the Justia.com website (Vanginderen v Cornell, Factual background, Section C).

In the end, the federal district court for the Southern District of California found that because the printed information was deemed to be both true and accurate information, there was no validity in the claim of libel or the other concerns. The case was dismissed under California's Anti-SLAPP statute (a strategic lawsuit against public participation), which allows for early dismissal of cases with an element dealing with the First Amendment if the case is found to be meritless. The Ninth Circuit Court of Appeals affirmed the district court opinion in 2009.

At the time of the case dismissal, Cornell University Librarian Anne Kenney reflected;

> *I feel that this is a real victory for the library in terms of being able to make documentary material accessible. I do share concerns that individuals might have about potentially embarrassing material being made accessible via the Internet, but I don't think you can go back and distort the public record* (Steele, 2008).

The example here of the printed student newspaper is perhaps easier to justify in terms of the information contained within the original analog container. A newspaper has a process of vetting information from its contributors before it goes into print, and also has a correction process available in the scenario of the accusal of false information (which may have its own statute of limitations, a period of time that the Plaintiff claimed to be "re-set" in the publication of the digital version). The move of this information from its physical container of newspaper to digital is significant here in that the action opens up access and the ability to discover information to an entirely different level, however it does not change the fact that the information contained within was found to true through supporting court records.

## 3.5    OTHER CONSIDERATIONS FOR DECISION MAKING

During a question and answer session at the #w2a Collections 2+ session at the 2017 Digital Library Federation (DLF) Forum on the topic of the Right to be Forgotten, a scenario was presented of a takedown request that led to a great deal of internal discussion and debate in a similar situation to that of the Cornell law suit. The institution eventually honored the request for removal of the information, even though this action went against the practices and informal policies to that point in time at the institution. This scenario below will serve as an ethical consideration within the same type of digital collection that may validate exceptions. The removal of information here was decided to be the more compassionate course of action.

The scenario was the following: A member of the library staff was contacted by a child of an alum who had come across an article in the digital student newspaper archive involving their parent. The subject of the article was about a violent crime where the parent was the victim and contained some disturbing details about the crime. This was a shocking find for the child, who had not been aware of the incident prior to that time, and had placed a request for removal directly to the institution.

In this case, the institution removed the text of the name from the underlying OCR, yet retained the digital image of the newspaper as it was printed. The implication of this action meant one could read that article in totality through the user interface of the newspaper collection, yet could not search and discover the victim's name in this article as the point of personal information. This decision does cause problems with regard to knowingly removing data from a fully indexed, searchable collection, however it was also the decision that the group felt was the most sympathetic for the sake of the privacy of the alum. I do feel that regardless of the outcome, we need to relay these types of decisions more transparently to the digital library users (point #3 in the 4 point privacy plan later in the chapter, adapted from George), in some kind of disclaimer or note that some content has been removed from the searchable index in exenuating circumstances.

Another interesting juxtaposition would be to compare the Cornell case with the Spanish "Right to be Forgotten" case that was mentioned earlier. In this case, the Plaintiff was successful in the request to have this information removed from search engine results, displaying the conflicting ideologies between American and European cultures with regard to this notion of the freedom of speech and the desire for erasure. Authors Kulk and Borgesius (2018, p. 5) reflect on the Spanish case: "Without Google's search engine, the newspaper announcement would probably have faded from memory, hidden by practical obscurity." In this case, the search engine was held liable as the "data controller"—the element that possessed the means to connect the user with the piece of personal information. This right to have personal information delisted from search results applied to lawfully published information, centering around the notion of personally identifable piece of data. Kulk and Borgesius find this to ultimately be a partial obscurity of information, pointing out there are other searchable elements that could also call back results without the one piece of removed information.

The notion of harm (or perceived harm) to the individual is present in all of these scenarios above, however this particular harm is difficult to assess particularly when the information is true.

As we can note in the 2017 Q&A DLF Forum example and the Right to be Forgotten court case, there are times when a more sympathetic, compassionate approach to decision making has been applied as factors are weighed after harm has been done, or observed by the individual.

The table below examines the core issues in Case Study #1, breaking down the perceived privacy violation(s), outlining potential concerns prior to digitization and actions taken. In this scenario, an alum was upset about the inclusion of a past criminal offense from many years prior that was including in a large digitization project to create a digital version of the student newspaper. From the institution's point of view, this project sought to provide online access to a publication from their university with full text searching, and legally took the proper approach through the digitization of the entire title (with support from the decision of cases like *Greenberg v. National Geographic*).

| Core Issues | |
| --- | --- |
| Perceived privacy violation(s) | Publication of content with personal name, in conjunction with factual criminal activity to openly accessible digital collection |
| Potential concerns prior to digitization | Creating a more immediately accessible version through the digital archive |
| Decision | Publication of the student newspaper in full |

**Case study #2: Reveal Digital & the Independent Voices Digital Collection: The Digitization Saga of *On Our Backs***

The publication *On Our Backs* (*OOB*) was a lesbian erotica serial publication that ran from 1984 to 2006. *OOB* was significant in that it was referred to as the first publication to showcase lesbian erotica created by, and intended for, the lesbian community. *OOB*'s run was relatively modest in print form, but held an important place within its community as a place to develop, define, and mitigate sex-positive discourse (Groeneveld, 2018). Further, the print distribution took place primarily within the trusted network and context of the lesbian community as the original intended audience.

In researching some of the background of the title, authors McKee, Albury, and Lumby (2008, p. 106) stated that "[Sundahl and Kinney] used Sundahl's earnings as a stripper to fund the lesbian sex magazine On Our Backs, whose title was a direct challenge to the anti-porn tendencies in the feminist magazine *off our backs*." The authors further imply that to that point in time, there had not been a sex publication that truly represented the viewpoint of lesbians, while many other underrepresented communities had numerous publications representing their community and collective voices more accurately. Colleen Lamos speaks to *OOB*'s particular significance at the time of first issue: "Born during the porn wars of the early 1980s, this San Francisco-based magazine straddles the divide between feminism and commercial (that is, male and largely straight) pornography." (Lamos, 1994, p. 88)

*OOB* was selected for digitization in a much wider project called *Independent Voices* by the non-profit company, Reveal Digital. The selection process entailed by *Independent Voices* included a consensus of scholars and librarians who chose and prioritized content into themed series that has been deemed to reflect an important piece of history or viewpoint. Through this process, *OOB* was placed into a series comprised of feminist and LGBT materials. The digital content was originally published online during the Fall of 2012, and later removed during the summer of 2016 (Reveal Digital "Statement about *On Our Backs*," August 2016[11]). Over the course of a year, Reveal Digital made a public statement regarding the decision to retract the digital collection, which will be also discussed below.

*Independent Voices* is a successfully funded project using the crowd-sourced digitization model in place at Reveal Digital. The series focuses on alternative press from 1960–1980 centered around themes of ethnicity, race, sexuality, and social dissent, including content from sources such as right-wing press, small literary magazines, and other media outlets. Reveal Digital purports to have the largest collection of such underrepresented content and presents complete runs of selected journals, newspapers, and magazines that fit into these specific themes (http://revealdigital.com/independent-voices/). *Independent Voices* is currently only accessible to the original funding institutions, but in January 2019, the entire collection will move to free and open access without any restriction.

Despite current usage restrictions, the consequences of publishing content from *OOB* were very real and immediate, in the release of personally identifiable information around sexual orientation contained in the original print of the unsuspecting subjects of the erotic photographs. Tara Robertson explored the personal level of privacy violations by interviewing women who had posed for *OOB*, and received some very powerful quotes from these individuals on what the transition of the publication from print to digital format represented from their point of view as the subject. One anonymous individual stated:

> *When I heard all the issues of the magazine are being digitized, my heart sank. I meant for this work to be for my community and now I am being objectified in a way that I have no control over. People can cut up my body and make it a collage. My professional and public life can be high jacked. These are uses I never intended and I still don't want* (Robertson, 2016a, Anonymous #1, Slide 11, LITA 2016, closing keynote).

Writer Amber Dawn spoke about her reaction:

> *What was once a dignified choice now feels like a violation of my body, my voice and my right to choose. In no small way is the digitization a perpetuation of how sex workers,*

*survivors and queer bodies have been historically and pervasively coopted. How larger,*
*often institutional, forces have made decisions without consulting us or considering our*
*personal well-being* (Robertson, 2016a, Quote from Amber Dawn, Slide 15, LITA
2016 closing keynote).

These statements reflect the very real, immediate impact on the individual as result of
the publishing a digital version of *OOB* online, a far cry from the original printed pages of
the analog container.

Erica Rand (1994, p. 192) described the moral conflict she grappled with on the decision to create a copy of a photograph from one specific essay in *OOB* into another analog
format. She talked about the decision about whether or not to have duplicated to another
analog format (slide) for the purpose of teaching within the confines of a single academic
classroom as problematic from her point of view, reflecting: "I also worried about the ethics
and politics of circulating lesbian erotica among nonlesbians." And further,

> *Nor did I ordinarily balk at showing images that generated discomfort, but I wondered*
> *how the dykes in the class would react. Would flashing our subcultural sex products on*
> *the screen or the predictable derisive class comments make any of them feel uncomfortable,*
> *unsafe or violated?* (Rand, 1994, pp. 192-3).

In the end, the author presented the concept of the original work without reproducing
the image from *OOB*, while she put in a considerable amount of thought and reflection into
just a single brief, temporary use of a selected image from the publication within an offline,
education setting.

Turning now to the legal aspect, the original contributor contracts in the Susie Bright
papers in Cornell's Division of Rare and Manuscript collections were illuminating in a few
regards as to the balance of legality and ethics (if there is one is to be found here). In some
of the contracts, "use" was granted for one-time rights for the print publication (Figure 3.1),
while other contracts spelled out the complete and full relinquishment of rights of all serial,
reprint, and anthology rights. The serial rights included in some of the contributor contracts
here define a clear use of the work by *OOB*, and unless specifed otherwise within the individual contract period, the copyright reverts back to the original creator. The process of
identifying the current rightsholder quickly becomes cumbersome to define across the various
versions of the contributor contract.

Entertainment for the Adventurous Lesbian

# ON OUR BACKS

526 Castro Street, San Francisco, CA 94114                                    415 861-4723

## CONTRIBUTOR CONTRACT

*Please review, sign and return one of the two enclosed agreements as soon as possible to the above address.*

Dear _____

We would like to publish your following contribution:

_____

ED APR 1 9 199

We shall pay you $ _____*30*_____ as compensation, within 30 days upon publication. We will not make plans for publication until we receive your signed agreement, so we ask for your speedy reply. We shall inform you within 30 days of when your contribution is scheduled to appear in a given issue.

1. You hereby grant Blush Entertainment Corporation (d.b.a. *On Our Backs*) ~~all serial, reprint, and anthology rights in the contribution,~~ as well as the right to use the contribution to promote, advertise, ~~and exhibit *On Our Backs* / Blush Entertainment Corporation.~~  *one-time rights only.*

2. You represent and warrant to us that the contribution is your own original work, that it does not infringe upon any copyright, proprietary right, or any other right of any kind, and that you have the unimpaired right to convey the rights you have granted us in this agreement. You also warrant that the contribution does not violate any local, state, or federal law or regulation. And you warrant that the work has not appeared in any other publication prior to this time, and will not appear in any other publication before its publication in *On Our Backs*, nor will it appear in any other publication for 6 months after it appears for the first time in *On Our Backs*.

3. If any actions, claims, lawsuits or other complaints are brought against the Publisher asserting facts that, if true, would be a breach of your warranties, you agree to defend us and indemnify us against any loss, damage, and expense (including attorney's fees) that we sustain because of them.

4. Two copies of the issue in which your work appears shall also be sent to you upon publication. You may purchase additional copies of that issue at a discount of 40% of its cover price.

5. We shall have the right, at our discretion, to edit, rewrite, condense, abridge, or otherwise change the contribution as we may require.

6. You shall provide a brief self-biography of 30 words or less to be printed in accompany to your contribution. You grant us the right to use your name (or pseudonym) and biographical information to promote and publicize the issue in which the contribution appears. Any pseudonyms must include a full first and last name, i.e., no initials or first names.

7. You shall submit model's releases in a form satisfactory to us for any recognizeable models appearing in your photography.

8. You shall provide an SASE if you would like the copy of your contribution returned. We shall use the same care for your work as we do for our own, but we shall not be responsible for its loss, or for damage to it.

9. If we do not publish the contribution within one year of the date of this contract, or if we cease publication before publishing said contribution, the rights you granted to us shall revert you.

Figure 3.1: Example of contributor Contract from *On Our Backs*, from Susie Bright Papers in the Cornell Division of Rare and Manuscript collections, Box 23, Folder 85.

Reveal Digital purportedly secured copyright permission in 2011 from "the copyright holder" (August 2016 Statement[12]) of *OOB*. The company had therefore assumed to also secure rights to digitize and re-publish online, although this was a problematic course of action for a few reasons. The copyright of the individual photographer/contributor aside (vs. the permission of a journal editor or whoever was considered the primary copyright holder of the title), there was not a consideration of the serious breach of privacy to each individual represented in *OOB* over the course of its digital publication. Groeneveld (2018) also found this highly problematic to also solely rely to the original contracts, particularly from a pre-digital world. The impact of a digital distribution point, particularly within a model eventually bound for open access, is vastly different from the original print environs.

In the first statement released by Reveal Digital on *OOB*, the company cites two main factors that led to the removal of the content; the first being the differing state laws when it comes to posting sexually explicit materials online and the second being the privacy of the individual contributors. Reveal Digital also goes on to state that digitization and posting of *OOB* is technically cleared since they have believed to have secured copyright permission (pursuant to 17 U.S. C Section 201(c) of the Copyright Act[13]) and go on to cite the *Greenberg v. National Geographic Society* court case as grounding to the legality. "Legal precedent indicates that publishers do not have to secure additional rights from contributors to digitize and display their previously published works" (August 2016 Statement[14]). The presentation of the legal aspect within their first public statement is a little befuddling at the removal of the content, especially in light of the two main factors that immediately mention the *Greenberg* case. The first reason provided by Reveal points to the uploading of sexually explicit material. This aspect that should have been considered at an earlier stage of the process, since the title is often referred to and classified as erotica, unless Reveal and its team of scholars were truly unaware of this aspect before this point in time. The second reason of contributor privacy is perhaps the more captivating to consider, particularly after content had already been released to a limited audience (and damage had already been done).

*But legal doesn't mean ethical....*

Legal questions aside, there has been some interesting research on applying ethical values at a more local level within the library (Robertson, 2016a; Vinopal, 2016; Robertson, 2018), and perhaps most importantly to engage directly with the community who created the content, or individuals who have high stakes or a vested interest in the project. To not reflect, engage, communicate, and successfully collaborate with the interested community is to further marginalize and alienate these same individuals. Both Groeneveld and Robertson call

---

[12] http://revealdigital.com/wp-content/uploads/2017/04/Statement-regarding-On-Our-Backs-20160824-Rev-1.0.pdf.
[13] https://www.gpo.gov/fdsys/granule/USCODE-2001-title17/USCODE-2001-title17-chap2-sec201.
[14] http://revealdigital.com/wp-content/uploads/2017/04/Statement-regarding-On-Our-Backs-20160824-Rev-1.0.pdf.

for a conversation point directly with the impacted community before dissimination occurs, as well as directly addressing the individuals whose privacy was impeded upon as direct result of publication of the content. A larger dialogue of consent needs to be present at the onset of project planning, and not as a reactionary after-thought after the violation of privacy has occurred. This process can be complicated to enact and adds another time-consuming piece to the project, particularly in examples where pseudonyms were used in lieu of legal names in *OOB* (even on the adjoining contracts).

Elizabeth Groeneveld (2018, p. 74) also reflected on the change of media from analog to digital having a great impact: "…the remediation of oob from print to digital form is not only a remediation of the magazine's content, but also of scale, audience, and interaction." In digitization and the dissemination of OOB, the content and information is transferred from its original analog form to a wider scale of access and consumption, far outside of the original intent and projected community/audience.

So what is the long-term significance and impact of this decision to ultimately pull *OOB* offline completely? We can look through many different lenses to consider this question, from all of the different vantage points from individuals directly impacted, to the institution and also of the scholars looking to access and use this collection. Does the eventual removal of OOB create a gap in research within a collection such as *Independent Voices*, or, conversely, are we beginning to make some considerations about the broader ethical considerations and practices to ensure safety and privacy on behalf of individuals (in this case, after the point of online publication)? Again, Groeneveld comments (2018, p. 77); "The removal of *OOB* from the Reveal Digital website thus prompts larger questions about what is and is not considered worthy of filtering in our culture and how social movements are represented, when pornography is excluded from the (digital) archives of those movements." The balance and conflict between privacy and open access is at the forefront in cases like *OOB*.

Of course, the analog version of *OOB* has been present in print at many institutions. For example, WorldCat lists 50 libraries holding the title, *On Our Backs*, although Cornell is the only one with a full run of the print publication (Groeneveld, 2018, p. 73). The printed issues have therefore been accessible to the extent that any analog printed media has been accessible for decades (i.e., in-person site visit or perhaps as a request for a print/digital copy of through InterLibrary Loan or other type of request). But, once information is released and published, private data is pushed into the online arena, and is difficult to undo potential damage. The concept of "freeing" information by way of publishing online in *OOB*, and weighing the sides of "All information wants to be free" against "Not all information wants to be free."

To specifically address the role of erotica, Groeneveld points to the element has complexities both ethically and legally (and, perhaps even at the most basic point of defining what does or does not constitute as erotica versus pornography). For example, some states require an age-based filter to be in place when pornography is present, although the argument on how pornography is determined is an interesting element here. And while the *Independent Voices* collection was under a semi-restrictive veil of access to funding institutions in the initial years, this does add a serious legal implication that did not seem to have been addressed at any level to date. Groeneveld further pushes the legal notions here in considering the aspect of sexual orientation:

> *It remains legal in parts of the U.S. to discriminate on the basis of sexual orientation. It is possible to lose one's job for participating in pornography. While in principle having free and open online access to a complete run of oob would be wonderful, a remedy to the problem of forgetting social movement histories, the reality is that not having to ask for contributor consent does not allow these folks the right to be forgotten* (Groeneveld, 2018, p. 79).

Groeneveld (2018, p. 77) also reflects on the mention by Reveal Digital to its detail of legal precedence within the public statements, if indeed the company was not technically in violation of any laws. And she further reflects, "Digitization practices occur within a wider cultural framework in which social inequalities exist, in which feminist and LGBTQ folks can be subject to harassment and threats, and in which participating in pornography remains highly stigmatized."

| Core Issues | |
|---|---|
| Perceived privacy violation(s) | Publication included nude images with associated names (both real and pseudonym) with aspects implying sexual orientation |
| Outline potential concerns prior to digitization | More awareness and consideration of the impact on the individual by the publication of nude photographs with peronally identifying information |
| Decision | Inclusion into digital initiative, published in 2012 (limited to subscribers), and later removed in 2016 |

**Case Study #3: Creepshot Subreddit**

> *Individuals use privacy to maintain their identity, but once information is released online, it can become difficult, at times even impossible, to control one's identity* (Davisson, 2016, p. 46).

The third case study presented here is perhaps the least conventional in terms of its status as a digital collection as compared to the first two, but I felt as though this was an intriguing collection of digital content in a publicly accessible forum (user moderated as compared to an institution or other originating professional organization as the overseeing project manager or content curators), and as such, poses perhaps even larger questions to ethical issues of a collective online, virtual society. In Amber Davisson's chapter entitled "Passing Around Women's Bodies Online: Identity, Privacy and Free Speech on Reddit," the author presents three examples of how issues of privacy and digital media conflict with consumption and distribution on the publishing platform of Reddit, one of which will be explored here (Davisson, 2016).

Reddit is an interesting blend of social media and user-guided content hosting in a social news aggregator. Registered users submit content (anything from hyperlinks to text commentary to images and other media), and the service has also been called "the front page of the internet." Other registered members then "vote" on content either positively or negatively, moving subreddits up on the page to reflect the higher vote counts. User-created boards are called subreddits and focus on certain topics, which have at times been controversial since the creation of the site. One of the few prohibitions of reddit deals with privacy, in the strict rule against doxxing,[15] or the publication of non-public, personally identifying information by way of the site itself. "Over time, society has ruled that a variety of behaviors—such as slander, copyright violations, child pornography, and hate speech—can result in sufficient harm to others to warrant a restriction on one's right to free speech" (Davisson, 2016, p. 45). Again, we find the conflict between privacy and free speech. Under the Reddit framework, there was a level of protection (albeit, temporary) of the original poster, and not of the subject in question. Further, each subreddit has its own set of self-imposed rules and standards, as set and enforced by its moderators.

I have selected the first subreddit example in Davisson's chapter to explore, but the other examples are equally intriguing to look at as ethical examples of digital collections in the wild. In the selected case of the subreddit Creepshot, Reddit users would load and comment on photographs of individuals in public scenarios, commonly with the application of sexual innuendos or other defamatory commentary. Creepshot also touted its right to do so with this statement, "When you are in public, you do not have a reasonable expectation of privacy. We kindly ask women to respect our right to admire your bodies and stop complaining" (Davisson, 2016, p. 48). Public and private worlds collide within the fabricated digital universe of the subreddit, forcing one to think about privacy expectations and coverage for both the subject of the photograph and the reddit poster.

After media outlets began to cover Creepshot, some contributors were identified and essentially outed (such as the Georgia schoolteacher who was found to be posting photo-

---

[15]   Doxxing refers to the act of searching for and later publishing and/or identifying private information about a certain individual, often with a malicious intent. The amount of information on the term "doxxing" on reddit is interesting in and of itself: https://www.reddit.com/r/OutOfTheLoop/comments/2e04kr/what_is_doxxing_and_why_is_it_used/.

graphs of underage students) that eventually shut down Creepshot, although subsequent similar subreddits have been created. Journalist Erin Ryan from *Jezabel* was one of the people who investigated this subreddit, and served to reflect on the ethical aspects in this scenario. And while Ryan does not contest the notion of the expectation of privacy in a public setting, the author poses the question that we should be entitled to fair and equitable treatment as a basic human right, and not be demeaned without one's knowledge or consent. And perhaps most ironically, the Reddit users who had posted under an alias and were were later publicly identified as posting some the most controversial photos were quick to cry for their right to privacy in their fabricated virtual identity behind their selected usernames.

Like Ryan, journalist Adrien Chen of Gawker did some detective work to unveil the identity of one moderator of the subreddit. The author insisted that the anonymity of the individual Reddit user was crucial to their own right to free speech and the revelation of one's identity would ultimately hurt the Reddit environment to an open and free dialogue inherent to the platform. This notion of the Reddit user's right to privacy and protection under the freedom of speech is richly complicated, since it has downplayed the aspect of the unaware subjects of the photographs who wherein have a lesser status or claim in denying the subjects' right to privacy by prioritizing their own right to privacy.

The Creepshot example is a different scenario from the first two presented, as the content exists within a user-moderated and generated forum. Perhaps what is most interesting to consider here is the presentation of reddit as an unpoliced, quasi-democratic place for opinions of all shapes and sizes, but how eventually the subreddit was shut down despite not breaking any of its rules beyond the posting of some images of individuals who were later identified as minors. I would argue that the same considerations we use as practitioners to think about privacy can be extended to other scenarios of posted content with privacy issues. These images did not have identifying names of the subjects as in the first two case studies, however other visual clues enabled some identifications to be made.

A lack of consent or awareness of the content by the subject, the context of image within a forum and application of subjective commentary to the images, and the potential of personal harm of reputation are relevant here for discussion. Can we also look at exceptions to the claim libel and slander in lieu of free speech? And who ultimately polices these virtual spaces? These particular types of hosting platforms are also moving targets within their self-regulatory mandates from a collective virtual culture and society. This case study is perhaps the most perplexing since the moderation of its content is under the control of vetted, unnamed reddit users who have claimed this level of power through their status.

Davisson ends the chapter with this pertinent reflection.

*Protecting liberties such as free speech, privacy, and the right to create and express oneself is a project so big it requires the participation of everyone involved. It cannot be* the sole responsibility of women to constantly police themselves to avoid harassment. *All involved must push for the regulation of digital platforms, the policing of virtual spaces to make them safe, and must constantly make the individual choice to not engage in the viewing, publicizing, and distribution of images that were not intended for broad public consumption* (Davisson, 2016, p. 57, my emphasis).

The idea of policing echoes the notion of consequence that we discussed earlier: who is ultimately responsible, and how can the subject regain control if there is a violation of privacy that is found, after the fact? These are largely unchartered waters in terms of finding a moral grounding and better regulating these types of spaces, and here we also come face to face with conflicting notions of privacy—that of the subject and that of the poster. Social pressure brought on in part by the media lead to the removal of the violating information, as was also present in Case Study #2.

| Core Issues | |
|---|---|
| Perceived privacy violation(s) | Photographs of unsuspecting subjects and adjoining commentary in a virtual environment |
| Potential concerns prior to digitization | Identify the right to privacy of unsuspecting individuals with defamatory comments |
| Decision | Self-regulated community, ultimately shut down after fact arose of inclusion of minors in photographs |

CHAPTER 4

# Core Values and Considerations for the Practitioner

Privacy, ethical decision making, and three case studies have been discussed thus far, and now I address how we can define some core values as practitioners and work toward improving the overarching dialogue and conversations around trickier situations as they arise. This will include a brief look at the role of policy, role of general counsel, and other selected Code of Ethics to be helpful in informing our work and professional ideologies. Finally, we will also touch on concepts of context, permission, and gauging harm.

## 4.1 ETHICAL DECISION MAKING AND THE DIGITAL LIBRARIAN

> *…when law fails to address important new conflicts and conundrums explicitly, it is necessary to resort to ethics to sort things out: to discern, for example, underlying principles of law and jurisprudence that might be invoked (in the absences of bright-line statutes, treaties or precedent) to guide our insights and intuitions on how best to confront the controversy in question* (Lucas, 2017, p. 40).

There are many points of decision making in any digital project, from the smaller tactical decisions to the more significant and substantial decisions with long-term consequence. From the moment of project conception to the final ingestion, there are many aspects that require decision making and often consultation with other internal and external constituents, such as collection managers, archivists, or other people with an investment in the project. There have been articles and books written to address many of the more practical, "nuts and bolts" components including digital production processes; from project proposals, digitization workflows, and other aspects, often with templates or other tools to help track larger decision making and agreements. The lesser talked about topics, however, have revolved around some of the murkier, less discussed territories, perhaps due in part to the fact we are still in the infancy of digital librarianship in some regard.

Defining and framing privacy in digital collections is an aspect without much in the way of guidelines for practicitioners; however, we must be more aware as professionals that adjoining decisions made as part of the regular work day can have immediate and lasting consequence(s). It is crucial that more research and conversations with the profession take place to address these issues more directly toward practitioners, and perhaps eventually there will also be the development of some systems tools to help assist with this endeavor, such as software that could detect certain agreed-upon types of personal information such as social security numbers that have a predictable format or context.[16]

We also need to work toward attaining fair information practices and policies; "Fair information practices… mediate privacy concerns raised by disclosure and subsequent use of personal information by empowering the individual, *even if people do not choose to invoke the procedures.*" (George, 2004, p. 175, my emphasis). Likewise, Helen Nissenbaum discusses the notion to discern an adequate level of privacy protection that is set by the particular context. G.F. George recommends that we move to develop a culture of privacy, in creating privacy policies, conducting privacy audits, creating education/awareness programs (both for internal and external "investors"), and implementing periodic assessment to ensure practices comply with policy (George, 2004, p. 181).

We can begin to do this, as suggested by George, with my adaptations.

1. Openly display institutional practice(s) and/or related policy(ies).

2. Provide users with a choice and a clear point of *opt-out*.

3. Transparency of practice.

4. Set consequences for violations.

(Inspired from: 4-point privacy plan, George (2004).

A higher level of transparency across the board is needed to assure users that institutions are abiding by good practices, and also serve as a way to keep ourselves in check, in displaying policy, providing opt-out, and showing end users our practices more translucently. And, as we noted earlier that the presence of consequence is crucial to successfully integrating ethical decision making, practitioners need to find a method that serves to dole out a consequence in some manner. The new General Data Protection Regulation in Europe, for example, sets a fine of up to 4% of a company's worldwide turnover as one method of enforcement in the policy (Article 79). Finally, Mason, Mason, and Culnan also highlighted what a "good information society" would look like:

> *Every society must find its place among a set of competing notions of good. A network of tensions exists between these goods, formed by the debates and arguments of people who want one end or the other, and each new social policy must find its own location amid this controversy* (Mason, Mason, and Culnan, 1995, p. 228).

---

[16] Interesting work reported in Woods and Lee (2015) from UNC on the notion of automating redaction of private and sensitive information in born-digital content in their article entitled "Redacting Private and Sensitive Information in Born-Digital Collections." And in a similar vein, Carpenter, Nichols, Polirer, and Wiener (2011) discuss the complexities in changing levels around classification in government documents over time.

This work is done on a case-by-case basis, examining the particular details and making decisions toward the greater good, although defining consequence here is a difficult task to define and implement.

## 4.2    ROLE OF POLICY

*Policies and procedures for gatekeeping serve to dam the leaks and redirect the flow to where it is ethically needed most* (Mason, Mason, and Culnan, 1995, p. 214).

One aspect present in many digital repositories is the role of the takedown policy. At times, this has been used within many institutions as a failsafe, providing a security blanket when objections are made to content that has already posted online and is openly available for access. Takedown policies can also serve as an a kind of absolution of guilt as to any wrongdoing from the point of view of the institution; something to point to as to address the potential of risk and violations within digital collections. The more effective takedown policies in digital repositories address specifics on how requests are reviewed and processed, and also which individuals are responsible for the review at the institution (Dressler and Kristof, 2019).

In the absence of a takedown policy, practitioners are faced with making decisions on the fly without a point of consultation, or devising ways to address requests as they are submitted. These approaches can often lead to inconsistencies in practice without having documentation in place to address such queries. There may also be a committee or working group in place at an institution to pose thornier questions to and gain perspective and agreement through consensus, although we need to build better networks of checks and balances to address these practices to ensure good practice. Likewise, a privacy policy can assist in the same ways as a takedown policy, outlining expectation and assuming responsible for good practice.

## 4.3    LAW AND THE ROLE OF GENERAL COUNSEL

*…while moral principles and the demand of ethics have the disadvantage of seeming ambiguous and open to a variety of interpretations, they function to discern order and protect basic rights across a far broader range of political and cultural situations than does the law, international law in particular* (Lucas, 2017, p. 87).

At times, the law is not always the source of ethical behavior, yet we often refer to examples of the cases that go to trial for guidance for practice. As in Case Study #1, the dismissal of the Cornell lawsuit has provided a reference for how the American legal system at one point in time considered a takedown request that was posed as a privacy concern. As highlighted earlier, this decision in the U.S. is juxtaposed with the Right to be Forgotten case in the EU just a few years later that began a revolution by way of a right to erasure for Europeans wanting to remove certain items from search engine results (more than 2 million requests to date with a 43% removal rate, as of the time of this writing[17]). Courts have the ability to later overturn decisions and make amends that conflict with earlier decisions, but the role of law can be quite useful when we do not have clear guidelines. Data protection laws can be implemented to assist in creating fair information practices. However, as we have noted, there may be circumstances that lead to exceptions at the individual and institutional level.

Partitioners at some institutions may regularly consult with their general counsel or legal representatives in times of conflict, particularly if there is threat of a lawsuit. These offices can be very useful to help advise and guide practitioners to make decisions that ultimately protect the institution from the risk of lawsuit, but may not always be in the position to speak to larger, looming ethical issues (Gilliland and Wiener, 2014). Practitioners can certainly work in legal advice as they weigh ethical matters, although there may be times that these two sides may not always come to an agreement.

## 4.4    DISSEMINATION AS DISCLOSURE

> *The separation between the information about a person and the person themselves through the abstraction process of commodity formation also separates that information from the social sphere of personhood which includes mutual responsibility, ethical and moral behaviours. Instead, data abstracted from persons and social relations is left open to instrumental use, operations of coercive power and outright exploitation. By design, such a situation cannot respect rights to privacy or individual autonomy* (Miller, 2016, p. 65).

Information of kinds are contained within many different types of analog formats. The information is elevated and released from its analog shape with the action of publishing online in digital format, discoverable through other pieces of information as inlets to access (metadata, transcription). As practitioners, we must address our role in the sequence of publishing information and take responsibility for the decision to publish, particularly if malice is detected. Authors Mason, Mason, and Culnan make a reminder of this responsibility of the individual; "Each party in the chain bears some responsibility for the decisions made on the selection and shape, color and spin given to the information. They are, in effect, part of the overall gatekeeping system" (Mason, Mason, and Culnan, 1995, p. 265). As the final gatekeeper between the analog and digital worlds, digital librarians must address the role of responsibility for the content and potential privacy breaches that have the potential to arise.

---

17 Google (n.d.) Requests to Remove Content Due to Copyright. https://transparencyreport. google.com/copyright/overview?hl=en.

Finally, the same authors also speak to the institutional responsibility; "…every organization needs to determine what information can or must flow to which people at what time, what information should not flow, who controls the valves, and how they are to be controlled" (Mason, Mason, and Culnan, 1995, p. 214). Practitioners are overdue to take an internal, critical look at current practices and the resulting consequences, and begin to create better policies for information practices. This idea of varibale information flow is intriguing, particularly if we better clarify the decisions about the types of information to restrict or conceal completely to protect privacy.

## 4.5    MOVING TOWARD PRIVACY NIRVANA? TAVANI'S PERFECT PRIVACY THEORIES

Tavani writes about the idea of attaining a perfect sense of privacy within the information network, through ideas of three different theories: a Restricted Access theory (where one has the ability to limit or restrict access to one's information); the Control theory (one having ultimate control over all private information); the Restricted Access/Limited Control (RALC) theory (distinguishes between the concept of privacy and the management of privacy; an individual can set up a zone to enable a person to limit or restrict other from accessing their personal info). While there are no norms in terms of legal or ethical to define and protect one's privacy, we can work toward setting the degree of control of information. This is contingent on three factors: choice, consent, and correction (Tavani, 2008, p. 144–145).

Tavani's factors are also parallel to the ones mentioned earlier that digital librarians can address more directly through ethical decision making in the creation of sustainable and fair information practices. We can work toward a framework that acknowledges and permits the individual to make a choice of inclusion by giving consent, and if required, make any correction in the event of information that is not true. This will not be an easy task—to better address notions of consent, awareness, and permission at the individual level. This process would be tedious and time-consuming work, potentially preventing or at least delaying the release of information, but is more sympathetic to the individual's right to the awareness of information, before the point of publication. This consideration before publication is the key takeaway, as "…individuals have the right devoid of intrusion or invasion, and to determine the usage, control and access of personal data" (Akpojivi, 2017, p. 271).

## 4.6    PRIVACY REVIEW IN REAL-WORLD APPLICATIONS

One project relevant for practitioners can be found in a publicly available checklist from the Ontario Genealogical Society (OGS) for staff members to track a privacy review at the *item level*. A privacy review is conducted after digitization, during the Quality Assurance process to ensure digital captures are comprehensive and in focus (OGS, pp. 3–4). Identified private information is redacted for the version for public consumption, which could include "…a line, a page or an entire volume" (OGS, p. 6). Documentation of the privacy review is made within individual "privacy sheets" that provide categories that represent the main concern by the reviewer, and are retained in print format with the original material.

The OGS privacy review includes identifying information that falls into one of six reasons for redaction:

1. biography of a living person or one who died within last 30 years;

2. contact information of a living person;

3. birth or marriage dates of a living person;

4. membership list < 50 years old;

5. photograph created after 1948 and either a copyright or privacy concern; and

6. other—any other item [project] coordinator feels should not be provided to the public.

Reviewers note the issue on the privacy sheet, with a brief summary description and the page number. There is also a column to indicate the year for follow-up and the year to open the content.

OGS's framework does imply a significant time of additional research into this process, by the inquiry into birth dates, death dates, date of photograph, or other knowledge impacting a privacy issue. The level of outside research can be quite cumbersome to delve through directory information and other resources required for such research and discovery, although it is hopeful to see this process in place within an institution to show that this is an attainable goal.

Another useful example of identification of private data can be seen in documentation published on the webpages of the University of Georgia. They have defined how to handle potentially sensitive, personally identifiable information within publicly accessible guidelines (University of Georgia, Policies Standards, and Guidelines). The guidelines were designed to help staff members who regularly interact and handle sensitive information in a set of best practices. Personally identifiable information (PII) at UoG is defined as: Name, Email, Home Address, and Phone Number. There are further definitions of *Restricted information*: Social Security numbers (including the format of the last four digits listing of a social security number), driver's license number, state identification number, passport number, any financial account number (such as credit card and debit card information), account password, and medical information. Lastly, *sensitive information* here is defined as: *any record* maintained that relates to students, prospective students, donors, and alumni, UoG identification number, date of birth, and any research information related to sponsorship, funding, human subject, etc.

UoG's policy also includes examples of the types of documents that would regularly contain sensitive information, and providence guidance to safe collection, access, and handling of any of the information listed above, as well as the safe deletion of electronic or paper files with such data. While this document is primarily intended for those in offices such as Admissions, Institutional Advancement, and the Bursar, such a guide would be equally helpful for the digital librarian to have on hand and serve as a definition at their institution as to what exactly constitutes as private data.

In addressing privacy audits within archival collections, authors Gilliland and Wiener compare an initial assessment to be akin to scanning a potential donation for preservation issues or initial appraisal. Further, they outline a process of even contacting a donor to assist in flagging potentially sensitive information, particularly if it is a large collection and/or is minimally described. They recommend taking notes as to where privacy issues are located, similar to the OGS method described above. And potential ethical questions that can arise from this audit could be the awareness of a donor as to private information existing within donated materials, particularly if the information is particularly sensitive or potentially damaging. Gilliland and Wiener also grapple with the notion of restricting information, especially when content is destined for digital collections. The authors frame these decisions by stating that we must "protect privacy while maintaining the integrity of the historical record" (Gilliland and Wiener, 2014, p. 29), which is an excellent way to frame the balance between open access and privacy.

## 4.7    SETTING THE STAGE FOR GOOD PRACTICE

*Context, purpose, audience, control, consent,* and *awareness* are main aspects that have been highlighted throughout this book, and important to apply within the context of working with both physical and digital collections. If these can be used as core values when we think about privacy, and begin to make determinations as to what would constitute as a personal data violation, each of these elements plays an important role in assessing a situation. We can be more diligient and mindful to the individual's right to privacy in the following: conduct a privacy review of material before content goes into digital repository; identify the situations where permission should be sought before dissemination; make some definitive decisions when redacted and make concealments (social security numbers or other pieces of data). The Appendix outlines some questions to apply at the onset of project planning to assist practitioners with these tasks.

We also need to identify at a collective level as a profession as to what constitutes as privacy concerns within our society, from the most egregious to the more overt, and what this implies to moving content into digital libraries in the name of access. In each of the case studies presented, there is also the concept of an individual's desire to retain control over personal information that can go beyond the narrow confines of which we have colloquially termed privacy, in a desired level of information privacy. "…when managing the acquisition, processing, storing, provision, and secondary distribution of information about individuals, the fundamental issue raised is whether individuals have a right to control information about themselves to protect their privacy, dignity and autonomy" (Mason, Mason, and Culnan, 1995, p. 256). This can be framed within the context of developing more solid, encompassing and humanistic digital privacy rights infrastructures with adjoining practices and policies.

This will not be an easy or simple task, in that it will need to provide necessary protection while not impeding on other rights and will require a new kind of digital landscape to be developed. As Miller wonders:

> *What this means for privacy and autonomy in its most basic considerations: freedom of choice and consent, the right to control our information, the right to control our property and likeness, the right to control our personal physical space, and the freedom from unwarranted intrusion or surveillance is still hard to discern at the moment. However, the sheer amount of data collected and the invisibility of its collection has the potential to make a mockery of the notion of consent, fundamental to our concept of privacy and autonomy* (Miller, 2016, p. 76).

The mention here of the invisibility of the actual collection process of data acknowledges the overriding need of transparency and acceptance of responsibility by the practitioners in their role as gatekeeper, as we move toward a more ethical frameworks.

## 4.8    ETHICAL DECISION MAKING: GAUGING HARM AND ACKNOWLEDGING RESPONSIBILITY

> *As scholars, as archivists, as humans, it is our responsibility to respectfully activate these records in the present, acknowledge the silences encoded within them, and bring them forth from the past into the future, ensuring that they will not be erased* (Caswell, 2014, p. 165).

To some degree, there is a certain level of inherent risk or harm resulting from decision making within almost every project. Within the digital library context, the decision boils down to whether to publish information of all kinds openly or not. The decision in and of itself has a very real and direct impact on the individuals with personal information included in the content, and we often have to find the balance ethically as to how to proceed in trickier circumstances with no clear indications in some cases as to the greater good.

The individual can view private information very differently than the institution may view the same information (Case Study #1). And at times, there can be a balance between access and scholarship while respecting individual privacy rights (Case Study #2). Other times, we have to decide whose privacy preveils: the subject or the poster of content (Case Study #3). We have been charged as the gatekeepers of collections and information, informally tasked with making socially responsible decisions on whether to push content from the analog context into the digital. The risk comes from the increased awareness of shared, networked information. "Every digital repository exposes an organization to some level of legal risk, in part because one of a repository's primary purposes is to encourage the collection of an organization's digital artifacts" (Reese and Banerjee, 2008, p. 222). And outside of accepting the risk of publishing private information, there is also the necessary investment of time and staffing in a lengthy privacy review process as a move toward a more fair information practice and policy.

## 4.9    PRIVACY ASSESSMENT AND REVIEW

We have talked about the necessity of defining better practices around assessing privacy in a more focused, purposeful review. Such a review can be found in Strauß's privacy impact assessment (PIA), which provides a framework to identify potential issues and risk. As Strauß states; "A distinction between different privacy types provides a more detailed picture of how privacy is affected, thereby facilitating the selection of appropriate measures of protection." (Strauß, 2017a, p.147) When this is joined with an ethical decision framework such as Curtin or DeWolf, we can begin to work toward a more thorough and systematic approach to reviewing privacy on a larger scale.

Strauß (2017b, pp. 146–147) poses the following questions during a privacy impact assessment.

1.  Identify pieces of information/data, and how is it processed?

2.  Is there third party involvement?

3.  What is the lifecycle of the information?

4.  What info is collected, and how is it being used and protected?

5.  What are the risks and likelihood of risk?

6.  Recommendation for existing or new controls to protect against risk?

7.  Documentation of risk resolution and residual risks (retaining a PIA report).

The questions outline elements around processing, risk, and lifecycle, which are also key issues that may be currently overlooked. The documentation of decision and risk is also an important one to note in Strauß's assessment.

Applying privacy assessments and reviews into production workflows is essential, but also quite burdensome. Particularly in mass digitization projects that by nature have a large volume of content would mean a review of any consequence of privacy would be exceedingly difficult, particularly in institutions with skeletal staffing on digital projects. However, this should not be an excuse for institutions to dodge the more problematic situations. We must take steps as a profession to make ourselves more accountable for decisions that have the potential for impacting the individual through the disclosure, purposeful or not, of private information in digital collections.

## 4.10    FUTURE DIRECTIONS AND CONCLUSION: MORALS, TRANSPARENCY, AND PARTICIPATION

> *[some people] believe (quite correctly) that understandings of what moral principles are and of what constitutes moral behavior vary among individuals and cultures, as well as in different practices or professions, such as business, healthcare, or the military, or rooted in religious beliefs that also vary among individuals or cultures. From this diversity of moral beliefs and opinions, however, they derive the conclusion that there are, finally, no "universal" moral principles according to which we all should try to live* (Lucas, 2017, p. 36).

Over the past few decades, digital librarians have built up digital collections, created best practices, benchmarks, and workflows for many parts of the production and post-production processes, although some ethical aspects of this work have yet to catch up to growing collections of content. The consequence of the role of the practitioner, the information itself and the adjoining technology reach a crisis when we encounter these ethical conundrums, however disastrous or benign. Not all information may want to be free, under the conditional societal elements that we need to work toward defining more holistically and compassionately.

> *Despite our lack of (formal) expertise, we are forced, whether we like it or not, to recognize and come to grips with the ethical dimensions and challenges evoked by these new technologies. In my terms, we must all become ethicists—and I will argue, ultimately, philosophers.* (Ess, 2016, p. 308).

As Ess states, we may not all be well versed in the area of ethics, but we may be put in a situation that calls for us to better understand the overriding principles and considerations present to make moral decisions. Whatever ethical framework or viewpoint we consider, we must also acknowledge our role and responsibility in the situation. As digital librarians, we are the ultimate gatekeepers to digital collections, the ones who ingest, index, and ultimately publish content to a much larger audience than the offline analog version would afford. Through the technological tools and means, we can unlock content through this act of publication, creating openly accessible collections but, in doing so, also open the potential for both positive and negative effects of this action. Using Heidegger's logic, humans are the elements that spur the action with the use of technology, and are as such, responsible of that recourse as the active agent.

There is an unknown that is present in the potential use or misuse of the information that we manage and publish. We set the stage for increased access and discovery, depending on the connotation could be either beneficial or detrimental.

> *We face critical decisions as a society and as individuals about how to rebuild memory systems and practices to suit an economy of information abundance. It is rare that any generation is called upon to shape so much of the world that future generations will inherit* (Smith Rumsey, 2016, p. 13).

I think if asked, most people would like say that that they always strive to make the most virtuous and morally correct decisions daily when applied locally, but we have seen that this is not always the case through the three scenarios presented earlier (although often these decisions were not for malicious reasons). We need to be more mindful of both the information and our role in the process of dissemination, with conditions that allow for growth as we will continue to question and update our own frameworks of morality and decision making. We must also be aware of the changing nature of society, in the overarching moral rights and wrongs, as these will have an impact on decisions. The ethical frameworks will ultimately shift over time as society moves forward and technology continues to make advances. If these decisions are made collaboratively within trusted networks of professionals using frameworks of decision trees and other documentation, we can start to think more critically about privacy and apply ethical theory by way of more comprehensive and informed decision making.

# Appendix

## PRIVACY FRAMEWORK

A. Questions to be posed to the original item or collection (digital or analog):

    1. What was the original *context* of the information/collection?

    2. What was the original *purpose* of the information/collection?

    3. Who was the original *audience* of the information/collection?

Do the answers from Section A inform and impact the public levels of access or restriction to the information?

Are there alternate paths to enable some level of access through redaction or other restrictions?

B. Questions to be posed to the notion of the original content creator (if known), or directly toward the information itself:

    1. Who retains *control* of the information (or perhaps more importantly, who should)?

    2. Does *consent* need to be attained before disseminating information broadly?

    3. What level of *awareness* has been made to any constituents as to the planned publication and distribution of the information?

Do the answers from Section B inform and impact decisions on levels of access or restriction to the information?

Are there alternate paths to enable some level of access through redaction or other restrictions?

# Bibliography

Akmon, D. (2010). Only with your permission: How rights holders respond (or don't respond) to requests to display archival materials online. *Archival Science* 10(1), 45–64. DOI: 10.1007/s10502-010-9116-z. 1

Akpojivi, U. (2017). Rethinking information privacy in a "connected" world. In Mhiripir, N. A. and Chari, T. (Eds.), *Media Law, Ethics, and Policy in the Digital Age*. Hershey, PA: GI Global. DOI: 10.4018/978-1-5225-2095-5.ch015. 14, 21, 29, 65

American Institute for Conservation of Historic and Artistic Works. (2015). Code of Ethics and Guidelines for Practice. Retrieved from: http://www.conservation-us.org/our-organizations/association-(aic)/governance/code-of-ethics-and-guidelines-for-practice#.Wdy8C1tSyM8.

American Library Association (2008). Code of Ethics. Retrieved from: http://www.ala.org/tools/ethics. 34

American Library Association (2014). Privacy Tool Kit. Retrieved from: http://www.ala.org/advocacy/privacy/toolkit.

Association of Computing Machinery (1992). Code of Ethics. Retrieved from: https://www.acm.org/about-acm/acm-code-of-ethics-and-professional-conduct. 35

Benedict, K. (2003). *Ethics and the Archival Profession: Introduction and Case Studies*. Chicago: Society of American Archivists. xix, 1, 6, 34

Berthoud, H., Barton J., Brett, J., Darms, L., Fox, V., Freedman, J., LaSuprema Hecker, J., Karabaic, L., Kauffman, R., McElroy, K., Miller, M., Moody, H., Vachon, J., Veitch, M., Williams, C., and Wooten, K. (2015). Zine Librarians Code of Ethics. Retrieved from: http://zinelibraries.info/code-of-ethics/.

Bingo, S. (2011). Of provenance and privacy: Using contextual integrity to define third-party privacy. *American Archivist* 74: 506–521. DOI: 10.17723/aarc.74.2.55132839256116n4. xix, 34

Browning, R. (1932). *The Poems of Robert Browning: Dramatic Lyrics, Dramatic Romances, Dramas Men and Women, Pauline, Paracelsus Christmas Eve and Easter-Day, Sordello and Dramatis Personae*. London: Oxford University Press. 6

Buchanan, E. (2002). Ethical decision making and Internet research. Retrieved from: https://aoir. org/reports/ethics2.pdf.

Cage, D. (2004). *On Our Backs Guide to Lesbian Sex*. Los Angeles, CA: Alyson Publications.

Carpenter, W. C., Nichols, C. S., Polirer, A., and Wiener, J. A. (2011). Exploring the evolution of access: Classified, privacy, and propietary restrictions. *American Archivist* 74, 1–25. DOI: 10.17723/aarc.74.suppl-1.p61prj6p86851l53. 62

Caswell, M. (2014). *Archiving the Unspeakable: Silence, Memory and the Photographic record in Cambodia*. Madison: University of Wisconsin Press. 13, 68

Chmara, T. (2009). *Privacy and Confidentiality Issues: A Guide for Libraries and their Lawyers*. Chicago: IL: American Library Association. 9

Clark, R. (2006). What's Privacy? Workshop at the Australian Law Reform Commission, July 28, 2006. Retrieved from: http://www.rogerclarke.com/DV/Privacy.html. 7, 8

Copp, D. (Ed.) (2006). *The Oxford Handbook of Ethical Theory*. Oxford, UK:Oxford University Press.

Curtin, L. (1978). A proposed critical model for ethical analysis. *Nursing Forum* 17(1), 12–17. DOI: 10.1111/j.1744-6198.1978.tb01254.x. 30, 32

Davis, F. (1959). What do we mean by a right to privacy? *South Dakota Law Review* 4, 1–24. 10

Davisson, A. (2016). Passing around women's bodies online: Identify, privacy, and free speech on Reddit. In Davisson, A. and Booth, A. (Eds)., *Controversies in Digital Ethics*. New York: Bloomsbury Academic. 26, 56, 57, 59

Deegan, M. and Tanner, S. (2002). *Digital Futures: Strategies for the Information Age*. Neal-Schuman Publishers, Inc. 5

Dempsey, L. (2008). Reconfiguring the library systems environment. *portal: Libraries and the Academy* 8 (2), 111–20. DOI: 10.1353/pla.2008.0016. 5

DeWolf, M. S. (1989). Ethical decision making. *Seminars in Oncology Nursing*, 5 (2), 77–81. DOI: 10.1016/0749-2081(89)90063-6. 29, 31, 32

Dressler, V. and Kristof, C. (2019). The right to be forgotten and implications on digital collections: A survey of ARL member institutions on practice and policy. *College and Research Library Journal*. Preprint available: https://crl.acrl.org/index.php/crl/article/view/16890/18536. 63

Dutch Data Protection Authority (2016). Dutch Personal Data Protection Act (English translation). Retrieved from: https://www.akd.nl/t/Documents/17-03-2016_ENG_Wet-bescherming-persoonsgegevens.pdf . 16

Ess, C. M. (2016). Afterword: ethics- and emancipation- for the rest of us? In Davisson, A.and Booth, A. (Eds.), *Controversies in Digital Ethics*. New York: Bloomsbury Academic. 70

European Parliament Council (1995). Directive 95/46/EC. Directive on the protection of individuals with regard to the processing of personal data and on the free movement of such data. The *Official Journal of the European Union*, L281, pp. 31–50. 16, 43

Freedom of Information Act (January 21, 2009). 5 U.S.C. § 552. 45

Freeman, L. and Peace, G. (2005). *Information Ethics: Privacy and Intellectual Property*. Hershey, PA: Information Science Publications. DOI: 10.4018/978-1-59140-491-0. 6

Frické, M., Mathiesen, K., and Falls, D. (2000). The ethical presuppositions in the library bill of rights. *The Library Quarterly: Information, Community, Policy*, 70 (4), 468–491. DOI: 10.1086/603218. 9

Garde-Hansen, J., Hoskins, A., and Reading, A. [eds.] (2009). *Save As… Digital Memories*. Basingstoke, NY: Palgrave Macmillan. DOI: 10.1057/9780230239418.

General Data Protection Regulation (EU) 2016/679. 8, 62

George, J. F. (2004). *Computers in Society*. Upper Saddle River, NJ: Pearson Prentice Hall, pp. 207–210). 62

Giannachi, G. (2016). *Archive Everything: Mapping the Everyday*. Cambridge, MA: MIT Press.

Gilliland, A. T. and Wiener, J. A. (2014). A hidden obligation: Stewarding privacy concerns in archival collections using a privacy audit. *Journal for the Society of North Carolina Archivists*, 11 (1). 19–35. xix, 1, 3, 7, 9, 25, 28, 37, 67

Google (2014). Search Removals under European Privacy Law. https://transparencyreport.google.com/eu-privacy/overview?hl=en. Based on criteria set by Article 29 Working Party's guidelines (EU): http://ec.europa.eu/newsroom/article29/news-overview.cfm.

Government Affairs Working Group (Society of American Archivists) (2013). Discussion of the Boston College/IRA oral history situation. Society of American Archivists council meeting, January 23–26, 2013, Chicago, IL, Agenda Item IV.O. Retrieved from: https://www2.archivists.org/sites/all/files/0113-IV-O-BostonCollIRAOralHist_0.pdf.

Grand Chamber of the European Court of Human Rights (2015). Delfi AS v Estonia 64569/09. https://tinyurl.com/y9ezlcna. 44

Granville, K. (2018). "Facebook and Cambridge Analytica: What you need to know as fallout widens." *New York Times*, March 19, 2018. Retrieved from: https://www.nytimes.com/2018/03/19/technology/facebook-cambridge-analytica-explained.html. 12

Groeneveld, E. (2018). Remediating pornography: The On Our Backs digitization debate Continuum. *Journal of Media & Cultural Studies* 32 (1), 73–83. DOI: 10.1080/10304312.2018.1404677. 50, 54, 55, 56

Haimson, O., Andalibi, N., and Pater, J. (2016). Ethical use of visual social media content in research publications. *Research Ethics Monthly* (December 20, 2016). Retreived from: http://ahrecs.com/uncategorized/ethical-use-visual-social-media-content-research-publications. 35

Heidegger, M. (1954). *The Question Concerning Technology*, Vorträge und Aufsätze. 20, 23, 39

Henttonen, P. (2017). Privacy as an archival problem and a solution. *Archival Science* 17; 285- 303. DOI: 10.1007/s10502-017-9277-0. xvii, xxi

Hooker, B. (2010). Consequentialism. In Skorupski, J. (Ed.) *The Routledge Companion to Ethics*, London: Routledge. 28

Iglezakis, I., Synodinou, T. E., and Kapidakis, S. (2011). *E-Publishing and Digital Libraries: Legal and Organizational Issues*. Hershey, PA: Information Science Reference. DOI: 10.4018/978-1-60960-031-0. 6

Independent Voices website, Retrieved from: http://revealdigital.com/independent-voices/.

International Federations of Library Associations and Institutions. (2016). Code of Ethics for Librarians and Information Workers. Retrieved from: https://www.ifla.org/publications/node/11092. 35

Introna, L. A. (1997). Privacy and the computer: Why we need privacy in the information society. *Metaphilosophy*, 28 (3), 259–275. DOI: 10.1111/1467-9973.00055. xxi, 22

Johnson, O. A. (1958). *Ethics: A Source Book*. New York: The Dryden Press.

Klinefelter, A. (2016). Reader privacy in digital library collaborations: Signs of commitment, opportunites for improvement. *I/S: A Journal of Law and Policy for the Information Society* 13(1), 199–244.

Knibbs, K. (2013). What's a Facebook shadow profile, and why should you care? *Digital Trends*. July 5, 2013. 12

Kulk, S. and Borgesius, F. Z. (2018). Privacy, freedom of expression, and the right to be forgotten in Europe. In Polonetsky, J., Tene, O., and Selinger, E. (Eds.), *Cambridge Handbook of Consumer Privacy*. Cambridge, UK: Cambridge University Press. DOI: 10.1017/9781316831960.018. 16, 22, 49

Lanzig, M. (2016). Pasts, presents, and prophecies: on your life story and the (re)collection and future use of your data. In Jansenns, L. (Ed.), *The Art of Ethics in the Information Society.* Amsterdam: Amsterdam University Press. 43

Lamos, C. (1994). The postmodern lesbian position: On our backs. In Doan, L. (Ed.), *The Lesbian postmodern.* New York: Columbia University Press. 51

Lee, E. (2015). The right to be forgotten v. free speech. *I/S: A Journal of Law and Policy for the Information Society,* 12, 85–111.

Lown, C., Sierra, T., and Boyer, J. (2013). How users search the library from a single search box, *College and Research Library Journal,* 74(3), 227–241. DOI: 10.5860/crl-321. 5

Lucas, G. (2017). *Ethics and Cyber Warfare.* Oxford, UK: Oxford University Press. DOI: 10.1093/acprof:oso/9780190276522.001.0001. 39, 61, 63, 70

MacNeil, H. (1992). *Without Consent: The Ethics of Disclosing Personal Information in Public Archives.* Chicago, IL: Society of American Archivists; Metuchen, NJ: Scarecrow Press. xix, 6

Manžuch, Z. (2017). Ethical issues in digitization of cultural heritage. *Journal of Contemporary Archival Science,* 4 (4). 3, 13

Markam, A. and Buchanan, E. (2012). Ethical Decision making and Internet Research: Recommendations, v 2.0. Association of Internet Researchers Ethics Committee. Retrieved from: http://ethics.iit.edu/ecodes/node/6053. 19

Mason, R., Mason, F., and Culnan, M. (1995). *Ethics of Information Management.* Thousand Oaks, CA: Sage Publications. xix, 11, 19, 21, 36, 62, 63, 64, 65, 68

Mayer-Schönberger, V. (2009). *Delete: The Virtue of Forgetting in the Digital Age.* Princeton, NJ: Princeton University Press. xvii, 21, 40, 41, 42

McCallister, E., Grance, T., Scarfone, K. (2010). *Guide to Protecting the Confidentiality of Personally Identifiable Information (PII): Recommendations of the National Institute of Standards and Technology.* NIST Special Publication, 800–122. https://nvlpubs.nist.gov/nistpubs/Legacy/SP/nistspecialpublication800-122.pdf. 14

McKee, A., Albury, K., and Lumby, C. (2008). *The Porn Report.* Carlton, Vic: Melbourne Press. 50

McNaughton, D. and Rawling, P. (2006). Deonotology. In Copp, D. (Ed.), *The Oxford Handbook of Ethical Theory.* Oxford, UK: Oxford University Press. 27, 28

Millar, L. (2017). *Archives: Principles and Practices.* Chicago: Neal-Schuman. DOI: 10.29085/9781783302086. 6

Miller, V. (2016). *The Crisis of Presence in Contemporary Culture: Ethics, Privacy and Speech in Mediated Social Life.* London: Sage. DOI: 10.4135/9781473910287. xxi, 13, 34, 41, 64, 68

Mills, J.S. (1869). *On Liberty*. London: Longmans, Green, Reader and Dyer. 27, 29

Moore, A. D. (2016). *Privacy, Security and Accountability: Ethics, Law and Policy*. Lanham, MD: Rowman & Littlefield. 21, 29

Newman, B. and Tijerina, B. (Eds.) (2017). *Protecting Patron Privacy: a LITA Guide*. Blue Ridge Summit: Rowman & Littlefield. 5, 9

Nissenbaum, H. (2010). *Privacy in Context: Technology, Policy and the Integrity of Social Life*. Stanford, CA: Stanford Law Books. 11, 12, 40

Nissenbaum, H. (2016). Respect for context as a benchmark for privacy online: What it is and isn't. In Moore, A. (Ed.), *Privacy, Security and Accountability: Ethics, Law and Policy*. Lanham, MD: Rowman & Littlefield.

Ontario Genealogical Society (2014). The OGS Digitizing Project. March 2014. Retrieved from: http://www.fwio.on.ca/sites/default/files/OGS%20Digitizing%20Project.pdf. 65, 66

Pang, N., Liew, K. K., and Chan, B. (2014). Participatory archives in a world of ubiquitous media. *Archives and Manuscripts* 42(1), 1–4. DOI: 10.1080/01576895.2014.905234.

Papacharissi, Z. (2010). *A Private Sphere: Democracy in a Digital Age*. Cambridge: Polity Press. 7

Parent, W. A. (1983). Privacy, morality and the law. *Philosophy and Public Affairs* 12 (4). 269–288.

Privacy Act of 1974, Pub.L. 93-579, 88 Stat. 1896, enacted December 31, 1974, 5 U.S.C. § 552a. 46

Prosser, W. (1955). *The Law of Torts*. St Paul, MN: West Pub Co. 7, 10

Punzalan, R. (2014). Archival diasporas: A framework for understanding the complexities and challenges of dispersed photographic collections. *American Archivist*, 77 (2). 13

Purcell, A. (2016). *Digital Library Programs for Libraries and Archives: Developing and Sustaining Unique Digital Collections*. Chicago: ALA Neal-Schuman. 1, 2

Rand, E. (1994). We girls can do anything, Right Barbie? Lesbian consumption in postmodern circulation. In Doan, L. (Ed.), *The Lesbian Postmodern*. New York: Columbia University Press. 52

Reese, T. and Banerjee, K. (2008). *Building Digital Libraries: A How-to-do-it Manual*. New York: Neal-Schuman. 2, 3, 69

Reese, T. (2017). Rejoining the information access landscape. Presentation at *ASIST Midwest Regional Conference*, September 9, 2017. Retrieved from: https://www.slideshare.net/reese_terry/rejoining-the-information-access-landscape. 4

Richards, N. (2015). *Intellectual Privacy: Rethinking Civil Liberties in the Digital Age*. New York: Oxford University Press.

Richards, N. M. and Hartzog, W. (2016). Taking trust seriously in privacy law. *Stanford Technology Law Review* 19 (431), 431–472.

Robertson, T. (2016a). Digitization: just because you can, doesn't mean you should. Retrieved from: http://tararobertson.ca/2016/oob/. 2, 51, 52, 54

Robertson, T. (2016b). Not all information wants to be free. *LITA* keynote presentation, November 20, 2016. Retrieved from: https://www.slideshare.net/TaraRobertson4.

Robertson, T. (2018). Not all information wants to be free: The case study of on our backs.In Fernandez, P. D. and Tilton, K. (Eds.), *Applying Library Values to Emerging Technology*. Chicago: Association of College and Research Libraries. 54

Ruedy, N. E. and Schweirzer, M.E. (2010). In the moment: The effect of mindfulness on ethical decision making. *Journal of Business Ethics*, 95; 73–87. DOI: 10.1007/s10551-011-0796-y. 33

Ryan, E. G. (2012). Is a pervy high school teacher posting 'sexy' underage students' photos on Reddit? *Jezebel* September 9, 2012. Retrieved from: https://jezebel.com/5944669/is-a-pervy-high-school-teacher-posting-sexy-underage-students-photos-on-reddit.

Salo, D. (2013). Privacy and libraries slideshare. Published on October 31, 2013, *Lecture for LIS* 644, Digital Trends, Tools, and Debates. Retrieved from: https://www.slideshare.net/cavlec/privacy-inlibs. 14, 34

Schwartz, P. M. and Solove, D. (2011). The PII problem. Privacy and a new concept of personally identifiable information. *New York University Law Review* 86; 1814–1894. 15

Smith Runsey, A. (2016). *When We Are No More: How Digital Memory is Shaping Our Future*. New York: Bloombury Press. 71

Society of American Archivists (2012). Code of Ethics. Retrieved from: https://www2.archivists.org/statements/saa-core-values-statement-and-code-of-ethics#code_of_ethics. 34

Solove, D. (2008). *Understanding Privacy*. Cambridge, MA: Harvard University Press. 21

Solove, D. (2004). *The Digital Person: Technology and Privacy in the Information Age*. New York: New York University Press. xxi, 10, 14, 21

Solove, D. (n.d.). What is an "Education Record" under FERPA? A Discussion and Flowchart. Retrieved from: https://teachprivacy.com/what-is-an-education-record-under-ferpa-a-flowchart/.

Spring, S. (1956). *Risks and Rights in Publishing, Television, Radio, Motion Pictures, Advertising and Theater*. New York: W.W. Norton.

Steele, B. (2008). Libel lawsuit against Cornell University Library digitization project dismissed. *Cornell Chronicle* June 9, 2008. Retrieved from: http://news.cornell.edu/stories/2008/06/libel-lawsuit-against-cornell-over-1983-news-item-dismissed. 48

Strauß, S. (2017a). A game of hide-and-seek: Unscrambling the trade-off between privacy and security. In Friedewald, M., Burgess, J. P., Čas, J., Bellanova, R., and Peissl, W. (Eds.), *Surveillance, Privacy and Security.* New York: Routledge, pp. 255–272. 13, 69

Strauß, S. (2017b). Privacy analysis – privacy impact assessment. In Hansson, S. O. (Ed.), *The Ethics of Technology, Methods and Approaches.* London: Rowman & Littlefield. 69

Tavani, H. T. (2008). Informational privacy: Concepts, theories, and controversies. In Himma, K. and Tavani, H .T. (eds), *Handbook of Information and Computer Ethics.* Hoboken, NJ: Wiley. DOI: 10.1002/9780470281819.ch6. 6, 7, 15, 21, 65

Trevino, L. K. (1986). Ethical decision making in organizations: A person-situation interactionist model. *The Academy of Management Review* 11(3), 601–617. DOI: 10.5465/amr.1986.4306235. 31

United Nations General Assembly (2016). The Right to privacy in the digital age: resolution, A/RES/68/167, November 21, 2016. 10

University of Georgia (n.d.). *Policies, Standards, and Guidelines: Best Practices Guidelines for Handling Sensitive Personally Identifiable Information.* Retrieved from: https://eits.uga.edu/access_and_security/infosec/pols_regs/policies/sensitive_personal_info/. 66

U.S. Department of Health & Human Services (2013). *Summary of the HIPPA Privacy Rule.* Retrieved from: https://www.hhs.gov/hipaa/for-professionals/privacy/laws-regulations/index.html.

Vaidhyanathan, S. (2011). *The Googlization of Everything.* Berkeley: University of California Press. 22

van den Herik, J. and de Laa, C. (2016). The future of ethical decisions made by computers. In Jansenns, L. (Ed.), *The Art of Ethics in the Information Society: Mind You.* Amsterdam: Amsterdam University Press. 23

van der Sloot, B. (2016). Privacy as a tactic of norm evasion, or why the question as to the value of privacy is fruitless. In Jansenns, L. (Ed.), *The Art of Ethics in the Information Society: Mind You.* Amsterdam: Amsterdam University Press. 8, 37

Van Dijck, J. (2013). *The Culture of Connectivity: A Critical History of Social Media.* Oxford: Oxford University Press. DOI: 10.1093/acprof:oso/9780199970773.001.0001. xxi, 21, 35

Vanginderen v. Cornell Univ. (2009). No. 08CV736 BTM (JMA), 2009 WL 33320, at *1 (S.D. Cal. Jan. 6, 2009), aff'd, 357 F. App'x 146 (9th Cir. 2009). 47, 48

Vinopal, J. (June 19, 2016). Tech-ing to Trangress: Putting Values into Library Practice. http://vinopal.org/2016/06/19/tech-ing-to-transgress-putting-values-into-library-practice/. 54

Warhol, A. (1985). *America*. New York: Harper & Row. 41

Warren, S. D. and Brandeis, L. D (1890). The right to privacy. *Harvard Law Review* 4(5), 193–220. DOI: 10.2307/1321160. x, xiii, 22

Weinberger, D. (2007). *Everything Is Miscellaneous: The Power of the New Digital Disorder*. New York: Times Book. 21, 40

What is the Streisand effect? (2013). *The Economist*. https://www.economist.com/blogs/economist-explains/2013/04/economist-explains-what-streisand-effect. 48

Wood, J. (2001). Ethical decision making. *Journal of PeriAnesthesia Nursing* 16 (1), 6–10. DOI: 10.1016/S1089-9472(01)44082-2. 29, 30

Woods, K. and Lee, C. A. (2015). Redacting private and sensitive information in born-digital collections. *Archiving 2015 Conference Proceedings, Society for Imaging Science and Technology*. 2–7. xix, 11, 62

Zook, M., Barocas S., boyd d., Crawford K., Keller E., Gangadharan S. P., Goodman, A., Hollander, R., Koenig, B. A., Metcalf, J., Narayanan, A., Nelsom, A, and Pasquale, F. (2017). Ten simple rules for responsible big data research. *PLoS Computational Biology*, 13(3). DOI: 10.1371/journal.pcbi.1005399.

# Author Biography

**Virginia Dressler** is the Digital Projects Librarian at Kent State University. She holds a Master of Art Gallery and Museum Studies degree from the University of Leeds (2003), a Master in Library and Information Science degree from Kent State University (2007), and an advanced certificate in digital librarianship from Kent State University (2014). Virginia has worked in both museum and library settings managing digital initiatives, specializing in digital preservation and digital content management. Her research interests include linked data, The Right to be Forgotten, and open source repositories.

Printed in the United States
by Baker & Taylor Publisher Services